Quest

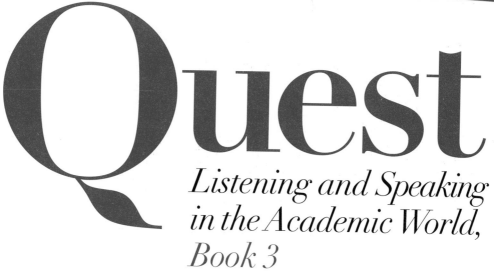

Listening and Speaking in the Academic World, Book 3

Pamela Hartmann
Los Angeles Unified School District

Laurie Blass

McGraw Hill

Boston   Burr Ridge, IL   Dubuque, IA   Madison, WI
New York   San Francisco   St. Louis
Bangkok   Bogotá   Caracas   Lisbon   London
Madrid   Mexico City   Milan   New Delhi   Seoul
Singapore   Sydney   Taipei   Toronto

McGraw-Hill Higher Education

A Division of The **McGraw-Hill** *Companies*

QUEST: LISTENING AND SPEAKING IN THE ACADEMIC WORLD, BOOK 3

This book is printed on acid-free paper.

5 6 7 8 9 0 QWF/QWF 0 9 8 7 6 5 4 3

ISBN 0–07–006255–2

Vice president and editorial director: *Thalia Dorwick*
Publisher: *Tim Stookesberry*
Developmental editor: *Aurora Martinez Ramos*
Marketing manager: *Pam Tiberia*
Project manager: *Joyce M. Berendes*
Production supervisor: *Sandy Ludovissy*
Designer: *Michael Warrell*
Senior photo research coordinator: *Carrie K. Burger*
Supplement coordinator: *Sandra M. Schnee*
Compositor: *David Corona Design*
Typeface: *10/12 Times Roman*
Printer: *Quebecor Printing Book Group/Fairfield, PA*

Cover designer: *Victory Productions*
Cover image: *Lonnie Sue Johnson*
Photo research: *Toni Michaels*

INTERNATIONAL EDITION ISBN 0–07–116389–1

www.mhhe.com

contents

unit 1
Anthropology   1

chapter two
Physical Anthropology   33

unit 2
Literature   65

preface

Quest: The Series

The *Quest* series addresses the need to prepare students for the demands of college-level academic coursework. *Quest* differs from other content-based ESOL series in that it incorporates material typically covered in general education courses, and contains a variety of academic areas including biology, business, U.S. history, psychology, art history, anthropology, literature, and economics.

    Quest has been designed to parallel and accelerate the process that native speakers of English go through when they study core required subjects in high school. By previewing typical college course material, *Quest* helps students get "up to speed" in terms of both academic content and language skills.

    In addition, *Quest* prepares students for the daunting amount and level of reading, writing, listening, and speaking required for college success. The three *Reading and Writing* books combine high-interest material from newspapers and magazines with traditional academic source materials such as textbooks. Reading passages increase in length and difficulty across the three levels. The *Listening and Speaking* books in the *Quest* series contain listening strategies and practice activities based on recorded conversations among college students, authentic "person-on-the-street" interviews, radio programs, and college lectures. Similar to the *Reading and Writing* books, the three *Listening and Speaking* books increase in difficulty within each level and between levels.

    The *Quest Listening and Speaking* books have been coordinated with the *Reading and Writing* books so that the two, used in conjunction, provide students with complementary, overlapping, yet distinct information—much as happens in a typical college class, in which students attend a lecture on a given topic and then complete textbook reading assignments on a related topic.

Quest: Listening and Speaking in the Academic World, Book 3

Quest: Listening and Speaking in the Academic World, Book 3 contains four distinct units, each focusing on a different area of college study—anthropology, literature, economics, and ecology. Each content unit contains two chapters. The anthropology unit is comprised of chapters on cultural anthropology (with a focus on shamanism) and physical anthropology; the literature unit contains one chapter on poetry and one on heroes and survivors (with a focus on the oral tradition). The economics unit is comprised of one chapter on developing nations and one on the global economy. The last unit, on ecology, concentrates on endangered species and environmental health.

    Unique to this series is the inclusion of three different *types* of listening passages in each chapter:

- Everyday English—an informal conversation among college students (or in some chapters, person-on-the-street interviews)—on both audiotape and videotape;

- Broadcast English—an authentic radio segment from such sources as National Public Radio and Public Radio International; and

- Academic English—a short college lecture

Unique Chapter Structure

Each chapter of *Quest: Listening and Speaking in the Academic World, Book 3* contains five parts that blend listening, speaking, and academic skills within the content of a particular area of study. In Part One, pictures, charts, and/or a short reading provide the basis for discussion and response writing and prepare students for the listening passages that follow. In Part Two, Everyday English, students listen to and use informal, conversational English related to the chapter theme. Part Three, The Mechanics of Listening and Speaking, focuses on language functions, pronunciation, and intonation; it culminates in an activity requiring students to make use of all three of these areas. In Part Four, Broadcast English, students learn to understand and discuss an authentic radio passage which, in turn, helps to prepare them for the lecture that follows. Part Five, Academic English, presents an audiotaped lecture on the chapter theme and guides students toward proficient note-taking skills; the final activity in the chapter, Step Beyond, involves students in discussion, original research, and presentation of their own findings.

Supplements*

The Instructor's Manual to accompany *Quest: Listening and Speaking in the Academic World, Books 1-3* provides instructors with a general outline of the series, as well as detailed teaching suggestions and important information regarding levels and placement, classroom management, and chapter organization. For each of the three books, there is a separate section with answer keys, oral practice, and unit tests. In addition, there is an audio/video component to accompany each of the three *Quest: Listening and Speaking* books. Tapescripts are also available.

Acknowledgments

Many, many thanks go to those who have made and are making this series possible: Marguerite Ann Snow, who provided the initial inspiration for this entire series; publisher for ESOL, Tim Stookesberry, who first said *yes;* vice president and editorial director Thalia Dorwick, who made it happen; editor Aurora Martinez Ramos, who gave encouragement and support and helped shape the manuscript; marketing manager Pam Tiberia, who guides the books into classrooms; Joe Higgins of National Public Radio, who went above-and-beyond to help us find one especially wonderful but elusive tape; the many students who have tried materials and let us know what worked and what didn't; the good people at Mannic Productions and Paul Ruben Productions, Inc.; the entire production team in Dubuque; and the following reviewers, whose opinions and suggestions were invaluable: Marietta Urban, Karen Davy, and Mark Litwicki.

*The supplements listed here accompany *Quest: Listening and Speaking in the Academic World, Books 1-3*. Please contact your local McGraw-Hill representative for details concerning policies, prices, and availability as some restrictions may apply.

visual tour
Highlights of this Book

Part One: Focus on Activating Prior Knowledge with Practice Opportunities in all Language Skills
Part One of each chapter contains a variety of high-interest activities that gradually introduce students to the chapter topic. In these examples, students are given the opportunity to think ahead by discussing with a partner whom they would ask for help if faced with the given situations. They also read a brief passage about what is a shaman. This section is typically followed by discussion questions and ends with a freewriting activity in which students share their reactions to the chapter topic or their knowledge of the subject matter. (pages 4–7)

Unit 1 Anthropology

...::::: **Part One** Introduction: What Is a Shaman?

Surui village in Amazon River Basin, Brazil

A. Thinking Ahead. **Pair** Answer this question: Whom can people ask for help if they are in these situations?

Situations	Person Who Can Help
They are physically ill (sick).	_____
They have a psychological problem.	_____
They have a spiritual problem.	_____
They need to buy a specific medicine.	_____
They have a family member who has just died.	_____

---

6   Unit 1 Anthropology

B. Reading. Read this excerpt from a book called *Tales of a Shaman's Apprentice* by Mark J. Plotkin. He's an ethnobotanist who traveled throughout the northeast Amazon of South America to study how rain forest tribes used the plants in their environment.

What Is a Shaman?

I was awakened by the sound of footsteps outside my hut. Koita had brought a visitor. The man was short—about five feet tall—but very muscular. His cheekbones were exceptionally high, framing his flattened nose . . .

5   Koita introduced him as one of the most powerful shamans in the village, and he did emanate a certain power—a strange mixture of the physical and the metaphysical . . . There was a certain dignity and a condescension . . . as if he would show me something of his healing plants only to demonstrate the superiority of his knowledge. Such was my introduction to the healer who would later appear in my . . . dream—the Jaguar Shaman, as I came to call him.

10   Traditionally, the most powerful men in the Tirio tribe were the chiefs and the shamans. The chief served as the ultimate decision maker while the shaman, or *piai*, healed the sick and maintained contact with the spirit world—responsibilities that usually overlapped. Illness was generally regarded as the work of malevolent spirits (sometimes sent by rival shamans), and the medicine man contacted the spirit world to diagnose an

15 affliction and to determine what special plants might be needed to treat it. The typical Amazonian shaman thus served not only as physician but also as priest, pharmacist, psychiatrist, and even psychopomp—one who conducts souls to the afterworld.

Source: Mark J. Plotkin, Ph.D., excerpts from *Tales of a Shaman's Apprentice*. Copyright © 1993 by Mark J. Plotkin. Reprinted with the permission of Viking Penguin, a division of Penguin Putnam Inc.

Chapter One   Cultural Anthropology: Shamanism   7

D. Discussion. **Group** Discuss the answers to these questions.

1. For what reasons might people ask a shaman for help?
2. The reading passage deals with tribal people in the Amazon. Do you know of any other societies in which people believe in the power of shamans?
3. Have you ever seen a shaman at work—either in real life or in a film? If so, tell your group about it.

E. Freewriting. In this book, you are going to keep a journal. In your journal, you are going to do freewriting activities. In freewriting, you write quickly about what you are thinking or feeling. Grammar and form are not very important in freewriting. Your ideas and thoughts are important. You will have a time limit of fifteen minutes for your response writing in this book. You can buy a special notebook for your journal, or you can write your ideas on separate pieces of paper and keep them in a binder or folder.

Choose *one* of these topics. Write about it for fifteen minutes. Don't worry about grammar and don't use a dictionary. Just put as many ideas as you can on paper.

- your reaction to the short reading
- your description of a shaman or a shamanic ceremony, if you have ever seen one
- traditional medicine men (or women) in your culture—from the past or the present

---

Part Two Everyday English: The Story
of the Shaman

Before Listening

A. Thinking Ahead. **Group**   In many cultures, there is a belief in some kind of good spirits (such as angels) or some kind of evil spirits (such as vampires or werewolves). Discuss what you know about belief in spirits.

1. In your country, is there a belief in ghosts? If so, are they believed to be good or evil (or both)?

2. What kinds of evil spirits can you think of? These can be from specific cultures or from the movies.

3. In your country, is there *widespread* belief in spirits, or do just *some* people believe in them?

4. Do people enjoy telling ghost stories in your culture, or is it *taboo*? Is there a day such as Halloween in the United States? If so, do people have fun on this day, or is it a serious time for **veneration** (respect) of dead ancestors?

5. In your country, is there belief in some kind of spirit that enters and lives in people's homes—a ghost or poltergeist? If so, what is this spirit called? How do people deal with a spirit in their home?

Emphasis on Listening Preparation

All listening passages are preceded by prelistening activities such as thinking ahead, discussion, prediction, and vocabulary preparation. In this example, students engage in a discussion about belief in spirits that will prepare them for the listening passage found later in this part of the chapter. (page 7)

Listening

Icons Provide Clear Instruction

All speaking activities in the book are labeled for pair, group, or class practice. Listening activities are accompanied by icons that tell whether the materials are available in audio or video formats (or both). (pages 8 and 9)

Chapter One   Cultural Anthropology: Shamanism   9

A. Listening for the Main Idea. **Video/Audio**   You're going to hear three students studying for an exam in their cultural anthropology class. One of them tells a story about a shaman. Listen to the entire conversation. As you listen, try to answer this question:

* Why did Brandon's uncle have to leave the house?

B. Listening for Details. **Video/Audio**   Listen again to Brandon's story. Then write your answers to these questions. Write short phrases, not complete sentences.

1. When did this story take place? _____

2. Why did Brandon's uncle go to live with the family in Korea? _____

_____

3. Was the family poor and uneducated? _____

4. What are *mudangs*? _____

5. How did their belief in *mudangs* affect the family's life? (For example, what kind of advice did

the *mudang* give them?) _____

_____

6. What did the *mudang* do during the ritual? _____

_____

7. What did she decide about Brandon's uncle (and what happened to him)? _____

_____

8. How did the family feel about this? _____

C. Listening for Inferences. [Video/Audio] An important skill in listening is the ability to make inferences—in other words, to understand something that isn't directly **stated** (said). Listen again to short parts of the conversation. What can you infer from each? Circle the letter of the answer.

1. How does Brandon feel about telling the story?

   a. excited; eager

   b. reluctant, hesitant

   c. nervous or scared

   d. happy

Conversational Listening Practice Featured in Part Two

In **Part Two,** students are given a chance to hear authentic conversational language on topics relevant to their interests and everyday concerns. In addition, these listening passages are available in both audio and video formats providing students with the opportunity to study the types of nonverbal cues that accompany oral messages. (pages 9 and 10)

---

10   Unit 1 Anthropology

2. Why do you think he feels this way?

   a. He can't remember the story.

   b. He doesn't like the story.

   c. He thinks it isn't a good example of shamanism.

   d. He doesn't want Victor and Jennifer to get a negative impression of Korean culture.

3. How is Brandon's knowledge of the Korean language?

   a. He knows just a little but is trying to learn more.

   b. He speaks the language fluently.

   c. He doesn't speak it at all but wants to learn it someday.

   d. He can have discussions about food.

4. What do Brandon and Jennifer seem to believe?

   a. It's important to call a shaman for advice before making a big decision.

   b. It's strange for modern, educated city people to believe in shamans.

   c. *Mudangs* have great power.

   d. There are many shamans in villages.

5. Why did Brandon's uncle have to leave?

   a. The *mudang* said he was an evil spirit.

   b. The family believed he was dangerous.

   c. He was an arrogant jerk, and the family didn't enjoy having him there.

   d. Brandon isn't completely sure.

Language Function

Telling a Story [Audio]

Most stories take place at a time in the past, so of course the storyteller uses past tense verbs. However, as you've just seen, it's possible to use the *present* tense when you tell a story. This is common in informal spoken stories. In written stories or formal spoken stories, it's more common to use the past tense.

Chapter One   Cultural Anthropology: Shamanism   13

Pronunciation

Reduced Forms of Words [Audio]

When people speak naturally, some words (and combinations of sounds) become *reduced*, or shortened. Here are some examples:

Long Form	Short Form
We've <u>got to</u> make a list.	We've <u>gotta</u> make a list.
She's <u>going to</u> ask for definitions.	She's <u>gonna</u> ask for definitions.
I <u>don't know</u> if this is a good one.	I <u>dunno</u> if this is a good one.
This is <u>kind of</u> weird.	This is <u>kinda</u> weird.
This is <u>sort of</u> weird.	This is <u>sorta</u> weird.
It was <u>supposed to</u> exorcise evil.	It was <u>s'pose ta</u> exorcise evil.
They <u>used to</u> call <u>her</u>.	They <u>usta</u> call <u>'er</u>.
She threw <u>him out of</u> the house.	She threw <u>'im outta</u> the house.

People usually *say* the reduced form but *write* the long form. The reduced form is not correct in academic writing.

Part Three: Focus on the Mechanics of Listening and Speaking

Part Three is devoted to providing students with listening and speaking skills that focus on intonation, stress, pronunciation, and various language functions. Here, students learn about the language function of telling a story, and the pronunciation tip focuses on understanding words that are typically reduced in the flow of speech. (pages 12 and 13)

Chapter One Cultural Anthropology: Shamanism   15

.·:¦¦ **Part Four** Broadcast English: The Jaguar Shaman

Before Listening

A. Thinking Ahead. Group   You're going to listen to part of a radio interview with M___ author of *Tales of a Shaman's Apprentice*. You already read an excerpt from this book i___ order to prepare for the interview, discuss these situations.

1. There are initiation rituals in many societies and for many reasons. Soldiers have t___ several months of boot camp, for example, before they become full members of th___ the United States, some college students **undergo** (go through) an initiation ritual ___ can join a club called a fraternity or sorority.

   Questions: Are there any initiation rituals in your culture or in your country? If so,___ group about them. What happens in the rituals? Who undergoes them? What are th___

---

18   Unit 1 Anthropology

A. Recognizing Parts of Speech. Audio Listen to each word in the context of two sentences. Figure out the part of speech and meaning in sentences *a* and *b*. You'll hear each sentence two times.

Word	Part of Speech	Meaning
1. chants	*a.* _____	_____
	b. _____	_____
2. scowl	*a.* _____	_____
	b. _____	_____
	(In this context, *fixed* means "to direct a look at.")	
3. alien	*a.* _____	_____
	b. _____	_____

Chapter One Cultural Anthropology: Shamanism   17

Listening

Jaguar

Sleeping in a hammock inside a hut

The Jaguar Shaman, a Tirio Indian from Suriname

Chapter One Cultural Anthropology: Shamanism   19

D. Listening for Reasons. Audio Listen again to four short parts of the interview. Write your answers to the questions; write just phrases, not complete sentences. You'll hear each part two times.

1. Why was Plotkin's relationship with the Jaguar Shaman an enigmatic (mysterious) one in the beginning?

   _____

2. Why did the Jaguar Shaman resent Plotkin?

   _____

3. What did the shaman appreciate?

   _____

4. Why might the jaguar be the symbol of the shaman?

   _____

E. Listening for Explanations. Audio Plotkin has said that he had an "incredibly vivid dream" of a jaguar. The shaman said that he (the shaman) was the jaguar. Plotkin offers four possible explanations for this experience. What are they? Listen again to one last part of the interview and write your answers.

Possible reasons for the experience

1. _____
2. _____
3. _____
4. _____

Authentic Broadcast English Featured in Part Four

The listening activities found in **Part Four** of each chapter are all authentic radio segments taken from a variety of sources. In this example, students hear a radio program called *Fresh Air* about Mark Plotkin's studies among tribal people in South America in an interview with Marti Moss-Coane on WHYY. The pages in this section where the listening activities appear include a shaded bar to indicate that the activities can be done in the language laboratory, at home, or in the classroom. (pages 15, 17, and 18)

Abundance of Practice Material

All listening sections in *Quest* are accompanied by a variety of activities that provide students with practice opportunities to complete before, during, and after hearing the passage. In these examples, students gain practice in the skills of listening for reasons and for explanations. (page 19)

. . : : ¦ ¦ Part Five Academic English: Shamanism

Before Listening

listening **Strategy**

Preparing to Listen to a Lecture

Most college lectures are fifty minutes long. In their lectures, professors cover information that is different from that in the reading homework, although they may refer to the reading done at home. *The more knowledge you have of the subject before going to a lecture, the more you will understand of the lecture.* The professor will sometimes confirm your knowledge (say what you already know) and sometimes correct it but will most often add to your knowledge.

A. Brainstorming. **Group** In Parts One, Two, and Four, you learned something about shamanism. Now bring together all of your knowledge of shamans and write it on the lines. (For example, what are shamans? In what parts of the world can you find shamans? How does one become a shaman? What do shamans do?)

_____

_____

_____

_____

_____

_____

Strategy Boxes Sharpen Students' Skills

Listening Strategy and Speaking Strategy boxes occur frequently throughout each chapter, providing students with practical skills that they can use immediately as they work on the different listening passages. These strategy boxes are always followed by practice activities that allow students to master the strategy at hand. (pages 20 and 31)

speaking **Strategy**

Synthesizing Information

One common type of question on essay exams is a **synthesis** question. In other words, the professor requires you to *put together* information from different sources—from the class lectures and the reading. If you study in a small group of classmates, you can share your ideas and learn from each other.

Example: A: Remember how Dr. Hicks mentioned the use of drugs to cause a vision during the ritual?

B: Yeah. I've got that somewhere in my notes.

C: Yeah! That's right. And Plotkin says the healer smoked tobacco and herbs. Do you think there was something hallucinogenic in that tobacco?

Listening Focus in Part Five: Authentic Academic Lectures

The listening passages in each chapter of *Quest* increase in length and complexity, and culminate with an academic lecture in **Part Five.** These lectures were written by content experts in each subject area and adapted to meet the special needs of English language students. A variety of activities accompany each lecture. In this example, students learn how to listen to words and terms in the context of sentences to infer their meaning and to listen for the main idea. The lecture in this chapter, *Shamanism,* was written by Professor David Hicks. (page 24)

Listening

A. Vocabulary: Health and Healing. **Audio** Listen to the following words and terms in the context of sentences. Each one has a meaning in the list on the right. Write the letter of the meaning next to the word or term it matches.

Words/Terms		Meanings
_____	**1.** at death's door	*a.* caused by drugs
_____	**2.** ailing	*b.* almost dead
_____	**3.** afflicted with	*c.* suffering from
_____	**4.** suck	*d.* person who works in a profession, especially medicine
_____	**5.** drug-induced	*e.* sick
_____	**6.** consumption	*f.* eating or drinking
_____	**7.** invalid	*g.* take into the mouth by using just the muscles of the mouth
_____	**8.** practitioner	*h.* person weakened by illness

B. Listening for the Main Idea. **Audio** You'll hear a lecture called "Shamanism," written by an anthropology professor. Listen once to the entire lecture. (You'll listen again later.) As you listen this time, don't take notes. Instead, follow along with the outline and keep this question in mind:

• What are shamans, and how do they work?

Emphasis on Note-Taking Skills

Quest offers intensive note-taking practice to accompany each lecture in **Part Five.** Students are provided with structured outlines to assist them in taking accurate notes. Moreover, well-organized postlistening activities teach students how to use and refer to their notes in order to answer both general and specific questions about the lecture. (pages 25, 28, and 29)

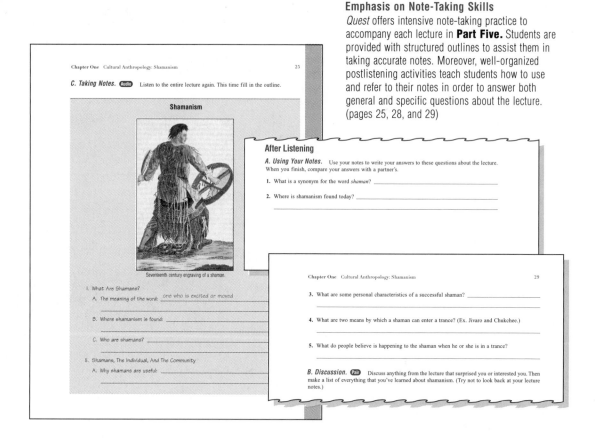

Chapter One   Cultural Anthropology: Shamanism   25

C. Taking Notes. Audio   Listen to the entire lecture again. This time fill in the outline.

Shamanism

Seventeenth century engraving of a shaman.

I. What Are Shamans?
   A. The meaning of the word: _one who is excited or moved_

   B. Where shamanism is found: _____

   C. Who are shamans? _____

II. Shamans, The Individual, And The Community
   A. Why shamans are useful: _____

After Listening

A. Using Your Notes. Use your notes to write your answers to these questions about the lecture. When you finish, compare your answers with a partner's.

1. What is a synonym for the word *shaman*? _____

2. Where is shamanism found today? _____
   _____

Chapter One   Cultural Anthropology: Shamanism   29

3. What are some personal characteristics of a successful shaman? _____
   _____

4. What are two means by which a shaman can enter a trance? (Ex. Jivaro and Chukchee.)
   _____

5. What do people believe is happening to the shaman when he or she is in a trance?
   _____

B. Discussion. Pair   Discuss anything from the lecture that surprised you or interested you. Then make a list of everything that you've learned about shamanism. (Try not to look back at your lecture notes.)

Academic Strategy Boxes

Found in each chapter, these strategy boxes prepare students to be active participants in the academic environment. In this example, students are given instruction in how to "psyche out" their professors. (page 29)

academic Strategy

Psyching out Your Professors

Students need to be able to predict what kinds of questions their professors will ask on an exam. Making such predictions (a skill that students call "psyching out" the professors) can guide how and what you study. (You saw an example of this in the conversation in Part Two of this chapter.) Here are some suggestions:

• Pay attention to what your professor *emphasizes, repeats, writes on the board, or appears to get excited about.*

• Don't be shy about asking your professor or teaching assistant what kinds of questions to expect.

• Consider what kinds of questions appeared on previous exams (if any) in the class.

Practice.   With a partner, write three questions that you might expect on an exam about the lecture "Shamanism."

Step Beyond: Chapter-Culminating Speaking Activities

Each chapter ends with a *Step Beyond* speaking activity. The content of this activity takes the form of a presentation, a debate, a survey, or an interview. It is based on the chapter's theme and incorporates the listening and speaking skills that students have practiced in previous sections. In this example, students first read a passage about a shaman's healing ritual. Then they synthesize information orally and present their findings to the class. Finally, they discuss questions related to the reading in their groups. (pages 29, 30, and 31)

Step Beyond

30

A. Extension. Ethnobotanist Mark Plotkin once injured his elbow when he was studying plants in the jungles of South America. Partly to find relief for his elbow and partly to learn more about the methods of shamans, he underwent a shaman's healing ritual. Here is his account of that ritual. As you read it, don't worry about new words. Instead, simply pay attention to the steps in the ritual. With a felt-tip pen, mark anything that is familiar to you from the lecture. Also, mark anything that interests you.

A Shaman's Healing Ritual

Night was falling, and the last shafts of sunlight filtered through the forest canopy and into the shelter. The shaman rolled a dry leaf of tobacco into a cylinder and placed it in a pipe made from the brown, woody, cylindrical fruit of the *po-no* tree, a relative of the Brazil nut. He then sprinkled several crushed
5 herbs on top of the tobacco. Striking a match from a box I had given him earlier, he began to smoke the tobacco mixture as he sat down beside me. The musty smell of tobacco mixed with the sweet-smelling aromatic herbs filled the small shelter. With his right hand, he gently shut my eyes and then started to intone a series of chants in order to invoke the spirits (according to the explanation Boss later provided). A
10 period of quiet then ensued as he awaited the arrival of the powers he had summoned. After a while, I heard one of the walls of the hut begin to shake violently as if something or someone were passing through. Then the shaman moaned and began a dialogue between himself and a being that seemed to be speaking through him. This continued for what seemed like hours. I slowly drifted into a dreamlike trance,
15 feeling as if I were sinking deeper and deeper into an enormous featherbed. Suddenly the wall shook again as if our visitor had departed. Silence enveloped us; then I heard the sound of a match being struck and the shaman relit his pipe. He gently took hold of my left wrist and raised my arm, then blew the magical smoke onto my elbow and massaged the area with his thumb. This was repeated three times and then he rubbed
20 the area once more with the cotton swab.

The old medicine man began chanting again, and I felt my body drifting farther downward, like a dry leaf caught in the autumn wind. Down I sank until I felt myself come to rest on a gentle bed of moss. Then I floated up to the top of the hut; from there, I looked down and saw the shaman blowing tobacco smoke over my prone body.
25 The shaman resumed his chanting and I felt myself drifting back down to the floor of the hut. The next thing I remember was him waking me gently by tapping me on the cheek with his fingers. He helped me to my feet; I felt a bit dazed and

B. Synthesizing Information. **Group** Analyze Plotkin's description of the healing ritual. Find at least four elements of the ritual that are familiar to you from the lecture. Work together to answer (orally) this question. Present your findings to the class.

* How would an anthropologist explain this ritual? What elements are typical of shamanic healing rituals?

C. Discussion. **Group** Discuss the answers to these questions.

1. What are the functions of a belief in spirits and shamans? In other words, why do many societies believe in the power of spirits and shamans?

2. What apparently "irrational" beliefs exist in modern urban societies, and what purpose do these beliefs serve?

summary of Listening and Speaking Skills

Chapter	Listening/Speaking Strategies	Mechanics/Academic Strategies
1	• guessing meaning from context • preparing to listen to a lecture • having questions in mind • taking lecture notes • synthesizing information	• telling a story • understanding reduced forms of words • psyching out your professors
2	• listening for implicit reasons • taking lecture notes	• expressing an opinion • expressing agreement or disagreement • softening disagreement • the voiceless *th* sound • using abbreviations
3	• understanding the passive voice • hearing rhyme and rhythm • giving a speech to the class • listening to a speech or presentation	• statements and questions • questions with *or* • responding to a negative question: agreeing • responding to a negative question: disagreeing • the medial *t* • making appointments/negotiating time • understanding common abbreviations • getting the main ideas in a lecture
4	• guessing meaning from context • finding a synopsis in the conclusion to a lecture	• starting a conversation • review: question intonation • reduced forms of *wh-* questions • the voiced /ð/ sound • organizing lecture notes graphically • comparing lecture notes

(Continued)

Chapter	Listening/Speaking Strategies	Mechanics/Academic Strategies
5	• managing a conversation • guessing the meaning of proverbs from context • listening for supporting statistics • listening for digressions • listening for quoted material • asking questions after a presentation	• tone of voice that changes meaning • giving advice and suggestions in the present • giving advice and suggestions for a past time • reduced forms in expressions for giving advice and suggestions • understanding Latin terms
6	• listening for indirect causes • listening to numerical information • reviewing what you already know/realizing what you don't know • giving a report from notes	• asking for confirmation • offering an explanation • tag question intonation • reduced forms of words in tag questions • choosing a topic
7	• listening to an anecdote • listening for topic signals • making eye contact	• answering the phone • finding out who's calling • taking a phone message • asking for clarification/clarifying • *can* and *can't* • recording an outgoing message • using a variety of sources and synthesizing information
8	• listening for emotions • recognizing figurative language • taking turns • listening to accented English	• expressing concern • intensifying concern • intensifying with stress • /ɛ/, /æ/, and /ə/ • memorizing

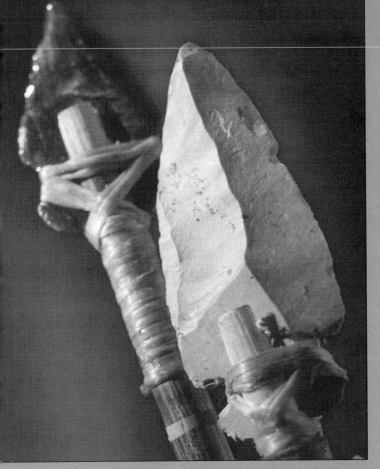

unit 1

Anthropology

chapter *One*

Cultural Anthropology: Shamanism

In this chapter, you'll read about shamans and how they work. You'll listen to a conversation, a radio interview, and a college lecture dealing with the surprisingly similar practices of shamans in different parts of the world.

Part One Introduction: What Is a Shaman?

Surui village in Amazon River Basin, Brazil

Amazon village in Manati Primaro, Peru

Palm-thatched
hut

A. Thinking Ahead. (Pair)   Answer this question: Whom can people ask for help if they are in these situations?

Situations	Person Who Can Help
They are physically ill (sick).	_____
They have a psychological problem.	_____
They have a spiritual problem.	_____
They need to buy a specific medicine.	_____
They have a family member who has just died.	_____

B. Reading.   Read this excerpt from a book called *Tales of a Shaman's Apprentice* by Mark J. Plotkin. He's an ethnobotanist who traveled throughout the northeast Amazon of South America to study how rain forest tribes used the plants in their environment.

What Is a Shaman?

I was awakened by the sound of footsteps outside my hut. Koita had brought a visitor. The man was short—about five feet tall—but very muscular. His cheekbones were exceptionally high, framing his flattened nose . . .

Koita introduced him as one of the most powerful shamans in the village, and he
5 did emanate a certain power—a strange mixture of the physical and the metaphysical . . . There was a certain dignity and a condescension . . . as if he would show me something of his healing plants only to demonstrate the superiority of his knowledge. Such was my introduction to the healer who would later appear in my . . . dream—the Jaguar Shaman, as I came to call him.

10 Traditionally, the most powerful men in the Tirio tribe were the chiefs and the shamans. The chief served as the ultimate decision maker while the shaman, or *piai*, healed the sick and maintained contact with the spirit world—responsibilities that usually overlapped. Illness was generally regarded as the work of malevolent spirits (sometimes sent by rival shamans), and the medicine man contacted the spirit world to diagnose an
15 affliction and to determine what special plants might be needed to treat it. The typical Amazonian shaman thus served not only as physician but also as priest, pharmacist, psychiatrist, and even psychopomp—one who conducts souls to the afterworld.

C. Vocabulary Check.   Find words in the reading passage that mean the following:

1. small house = _____

2. cured = _____

3. sickness = _____

4. bad, evil = _____

5. study symptoms to decide what disease a person has = _____

6. suffering (noun) = _____

7. someone who leads a soul to the afterworld = _____

D. Discussion. (Group)   Discuss the answers to these questions.

1. For what reasons might people ask a shaman for help?

2. The reading passage deals with tribal people in the Amazon. Do you know of any other societies in which people believe in the power of shamans?

3. Have you ever seen a shaman at work—either in real life or in a film? If so, tell your group about it.

E. Freewriting.   In this book, you are going to keep a journal. In your journal, you are going to do freewriting activities. In freewriting, you write quickly about what you are thinking or feeling. Grammar and form are not very important in freewriting. Your ideas and thoughts are important. You will have a time limit of fifteen minutes for your response writing in this book. You can buy a special notebook for your journal, or you can write your ideas on separate pieces of paper and keep them in a binder or folder.

Choose *one* of these topics. Write about it for fifteen minutes. Don't worry about grammar and don't use a dictionary. Just put as many ideas as you can on paper.

- your reaction to the short reading

- your description of a shaman or a shamanic ceremony, if you have ever seen one

- traditional medicine men (or women) in your culture—from the past or the present

. : : : : : Part Two Everyday English: The Story of the Shaman

Before Listening

A. Thinking Ahead. (Group)   In many cultures, there is a belief in some kind of good spirits (such as angels) or some kind of evil spirits (such as vampires or werewolves). Discuss what you know about belief in spirits.

1. In your country, is there a belief in ghosts? If so, are they believed to be good or evil (or both)?

2. What kinds of evil spirits can you think of? These can be from specific cultures or from the movies.

3. In your country, is there *widespread* belief in spirits, or do just *some* people believe in them?

4. Do people enjoy telling ghost stories in your culture, or is it *taboo*? Is there a day such as Halloween in the United States? If so, do people have fun on this day, or is it a serious time for **veneration** (respect) of dead ancestors?

5. In your country, is there belief in some kind of spirit that enters and lives in people's homes—a ghost or poltergeist? If so, what is this spirit called? How do people deal with a spirit in their home?

B. Vocabulary Preparation: Informal Words.   You are going to hear the students in the conversation use some expressions that are common in casual conversation. First, read each sentence and guess the meaning of the underlined words. Then choose their meaning from the definitions in the box. Write the letters in the blanks.

Definitions

a. irritate a lot

b. make (someone) go away

c. lot

d. invent; create

e. strange

f. stupid, foolish, or rude person

g. think; predict

Sentences

_____   **1.** There are a <u>bunch</u> of new words in this chapter.

_____   **2.** I <u>bet</u> the next test is going to be hard.

_____   **3.** Nobody else thought it was unusual, but it seemed really <u>weird</u> to me.

_____   **4.** It used to <u>drive</u> him <u>crazy</u> when we told that story, but it was fun to see him get so bothered.

_____   **5.** Most of the time, he's pretty nice, but sometimes he can be a real <u>jerk</u>.

_____   **6.** When I was in school, I used to <u>cook up</u> amazing excuses when I didn't have my homework. Some of my teachers appreciated my imagination, but of course they never believed me.

_____   **7.** When I was a kid, sometimes my big sister would give me money to go to the movies. I think she was just trying to <u>get rid of</u> me so she could be alone with her friends.

Listening

A. Listening for the Main Idea.   **Video/Audio**   You're going to hear three students studying for an exam in their cultural anthropology class. One of them tells a story about a shaman. Listen to the entire conversation. As you listen, try to answer this question:

- Why did Brandon's uncle have to leave the house?

B. Listening for Details.   **Video/Audio**   Listen again to Brandon's story. Then write your answers to these questions. Write short phrases, not complete sentences.

1. When did this story take place? _____

2. Why did Brandon's uncle go to live with the family in Korea? _____

_____

3. Was the family poor and uneducated? _____

4. What are *mudangs*? _____

5. How did their belief in *mudangs* affect the family's life? (For example, what kind of advice did

the *mudang* give them?) _____

_____

6. What did the *mudang* do during the ritual? _____

_____

7. What did she decide about Brandon's uncle (and what happened to him)? _____

_____

8. How did the family feel about this? _____

C. Listening for Inferences.   **Video/Audio**   An important skill in listening is the ability to make inferences—in other words, to understand something that isn't directly **stated** (said). Listen again to short parts of the conversation. What can you infer from each? Circle the letter of the answer.

1. How does Brandon feel about telling the story?

 a. excited; eager

 b. reluctant, hesitant

 c. nervous or scared

 d. happy

2. Why do you think he feels this way?

　　a. He can't remember the story.

　　b. He doesn't like the story.

　　c. He thinks it isn't a good example of shamanism.

　　d. He doesn't want Victor and Jennifer to get a negative impression of Korean culture.

3. How is Brandon's knowledge of the Korean language?

　　a. He knows just a little but is trying to learn more.

　　b. He speaks the language fluently.

　　c. He doesn't speak it at all but wants to learn it someday.

　　d. He can have discussions about food.

4. What do Brandon and Jennifer seem to believe?

　　a. It's important to call a shaman for advice before making a big decision.

　　b. It's strange for modern, educated city people to believe in shamans.

　　c. *Mudangs* have great power.

　　d. There are many shamans in villages.

5. Why did Brandon's uncle have to leave?

　　a. The *mudang* said he was an evil spirit.

　　b. The family believed he was dangerous.

　　c. He was an arrogant jerk, and the family didn't enjoy having him there.

　　d. Brandon isn't completely sure.

After Listening

A. Guessing Meaning from Context.   In the conversation, you heard some words used in anthropology. Guess the meanings of some of the words from the conversation. The words are underlined in the sentences. Look for clues to their meanings in the words around them.

　　Write your guess in the blank after each sentence. Compare your answers with a partner's. Then check your guess with your teacher or the dictionary.

1. There are still shamans in Korea, sort of <u>witch doctors</u>, you know?

　　Guess: _____

2. She used to come over to the house and check things out and perform a <u>ritual</u>.

   Guess: _____

3. She'd sing and dance and shake a <u>rattle</u> and maybe go into a <u>trance</u>.

   Guess: (rattle) _____

   Guess: (trance) _____

4. The whole ritual was supposed to <u>exorcise</u> any evil spirits from the house—clean bad spirits out of the house.

   Guess: _____

B. Collecting Related Information. `Class` Move around the classroom and interview other students. (In addition, for homework your teacher might have you interview other people in your school or neighborhood.) Find examples of **rituals,** the culture(s) in which they are found, the people who perform them, and their purpose. These can be from a specific country or from many countries. They can be religious or secular, traditional or modern. Some might be *rites of passage*—rituals that move a person from one stage of life to another (weddings, funerals, certain birthdays, etc.).

Example:

Ritual	Culture(s)	Performed by	Purpose
exorcism	Korea	mudangs (female shamans)	cleanse the house of evil spirits

Ritual	Culture(s)	Performed by	Purpose

C. Reporting Your Findings. `Pair` Tell a classmate what rituals you learned about.

Part Three The Mechanics of Listening and Speaking

A. Practice. (Video/Audio) In Part Two, you heard Brandon tell a story about his uncle. Now listen to the ending to this same story told in a slightly different way. Pay special attention to the verbs. Fill in the blanks as you listen.

So my uncle _____ 1 to Korea, and he _____ 2 with his cousins and aunt and uncle there. He's trying to learn the language, you know?

Well, the family _____ 3 the mudang over to check the house out. She _____ 4 over and _____ 5 her ritual. In this ritual, she's in a sort of trance. And when she _____ 6 out of this trance, (and this is the weird part) she _____ 7 that my uncle's an evil spirit, and he _____ 8 to get out of the house right away.

Language Function

Telling a Story Audio

Most stories take place at a time in the past, so of course the storyteller uses past tense verbs. However, as you've just seen, it's possible to use the *present* tense when you tell a story. This is common in informal spoken stories. In written stories or formal spoken stories, it's more common to use the past tense.

Pronunciation

Reduced Forms of Words Audio

When people speak naturally, some words (and combinations of sounds) become *reduced,* or short-ened. Here are some examples:

Long Form	Short Form
We've <u>got to</u> make a list.	We've <u>gotta</u> make a list.
She's <u>going to</u> ask for definitions.	She's <u>gonna</u> ask for definitions.
I <u>don't know</u> if this is a good one.	I <u>dunno</u> if this is a good one.
This is <u>kind of</u> weird.	This is <u>kinda</u> weird.
This is <u>sort of</u> weird.	This is <u>sorta</u> weird.
It was <u>supposed to</u> exorcise evil.	It was <u>s'pose ta</u> exorcise evil.
They <u>used to</u> call <u>her</u>.	They <u>usta</u> call <u>'er</u>.
She threw <u>him out of</u> the house.	She threw <u>'im outta</u> the house.

People usually *say* the reduced form but *write* the long form. The reduced form is not correct in academic writing.

B. Practice. Audio   Listen to these short conversations. You'll hear the reduced forms of some words. Fill in the blanks with the long forms.

1. A: Dr. Roberts is _____ give a test on the chapter about shamanism.

    B: I know, and I haven't even read it yet. I've _____ get busy tonight.

    A: I thought you were _____ help your brother move tonight.

    B: Oh no! That's right. I'll just tell _____ I can't. He'll be

    _____ mad, but what can I do?

2. A: When my mom was a kid, her family _____ live in South America. And

    one time some friends took _____ to a little Indian village where she

    met a shaman.

    B: Really?

    A: Yeah. She says she was really scared of _____ —especially when he did

    this ritual where he went into a _____ trance in order to cure a sick

    little boy.

    B: Did it work?

    A: Well, he got better, but I _____ if it was because of the ritual.

Review: Language Functions

Telling a Story `Video/Audio`

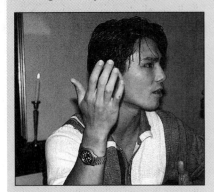

Listen to this example of the ending to an informal story. Pay attention to pronunciation and use of tenses; if you watch the video, also pay attention to facial expression. You'll use this function in the next section.

Put It Together

A. Planning a Story.   For homework, think of a very short story to tell a small group of students. Try to think of a story that is either funny, frightening, or amazing. Choose *one* of the following.

• a story that your family tells over and over

• a ghost story from your culture

• something strange that once happened to you or someone you know

• an unusual ritual that you have observed

Decide if you want to use the past tense or the present tense. Then make notes on your story so that you don't forget any points.

B. Telling a Story. `Group`   In class, tell your story to a small group (4–5 students). You shouldn't read from your notes, but you can glance at them occasionally to help you remember. To show interest or surprise when another student is telling a story, you can use these expressions.

Expressing Interest	Expressing Surprise
• So what happened next?	• Wow!
• And then?	• Oh my gosh!
• Really?	• You're kidding!
• That's great.	• You've got to be kidding!

. : : : : **Part Four** Broadcast English: The Jaguar Shaman

Before Listening

A. Thinking Ahead. **Group**   You're going to listen to part of a radio interview with Mark J. Plotkin, author of *Tales of a Shaman's Apprentice*. You already read an excerpt from this book in Part One. In order to prepare for the interview, discuss these situations.

1. There are initiation rituals in many societies and for many reasons. Soldiers have to go through several months of boot camp, for example, before they become full members of the military. In the United States, some college students **undergo** (go through) an initiation ritual before they can join a club called a fraternity or sorority.

   Questions: Are there any initiation rituals in your culture or in your country? If so, tell your group about them. What happens in the rituals? Who undergoes them? What are the steps?

2. Modern psychologists have several theories about the meaning of dreams—that they express our thoughts and concerns about daily life, that they are a way of solving problems, or that they result from brain activity but have no meaning at all.

   Questions: How do people in *traditional* societies interpret dreams? What did your grandparents or great-grandparents believe about dreams?

3. Various animals can be symbols of different things. For example, they might be a symbol of a country, a school, an organization, or even a person.

   Question: What animals can you think of that are symbols of something else? Brainstorm for a few minutes and fill in this chart.

Animal	Symbol of
_____	_____
_____	_____
_____	_____
_____	_____
_____	_____
_____	_____

listening Strategy

Guessing Meaning from Context

When you listen to a radio interview in English, you might not understand everything. If your goal is simply to get the main ideas, it isn't necessary to know the meaning of every word. However, with time and practice (and a clear context!) you should be able to guess the meaning of some words. This skill may be easier to practice in *reading* because the words stay on the page, and you have time to think. But occasionally it's easier to guess from context in *listening* because the speaker's intonation helps you. In this book, you'll practice both ways of guessing meaning from context.

B. Vocabulary Preparation.   There are words in the radio interview that may be new to you. First, read each sentence and guess the meaning of the underlined words. Then choose their meaning from the definitions in the box. Write the letters in the blanks.

Sentences

_____ **1.** The class that they call Anthropology 121 at Valley College is basically <u>equivalent to</u> Cultural Anthropology 151 at City University.

_____ **2.** Part of the cure for his illness involved <u>dietary restrictions</u>.

_____ **3.** When he swallowed the <u>hallucinogenic</u> drink, he suddenly saw his great-grandfather, who had died fifty years earlier, and had a conversation with him.

_____ **4.** People in the village believe that if they eat some of that hallucinogenic plant, they'll see a vision and be able to <u>commune</u> with spirits.

_____ **5.** She <u>resented</u> the fact that she had studied so hard for a B when I hadn't studied at all and got an A on the same exam.

_____ **6.** He <u>strolled</u> out of the village and left only his footprints behind him.

_____ **7.** He didn't seem to like my many questions. <u>By the same token</u>, he seemed to appreciate the fact that I wanted to learn from him.

_____ **8.** When I told him my story, it sort of <u>broke the ice</u> between us, and he started to be friendly.

_____ **9.** She was an uneducated child from a poor family, but she <u>turned</u> herself <u>into</u> a highly successful businesswoman.

_____ **10.** At the <u>outset</u>, the medicine man refused to show me many healing plants. However, after a while, he grew to trust me and shared much of his knowledge of the forest.

Definitions
a. felt angry about
b. beginning
c. exchange ideas
d. the same as
e. surprisingly, for similar reasons
f. created a friendly atmosphere
g. became
h. walked
i. foods that one isn't allowed to eat
j. causing people to see and hear things that aren't there

Listening

Jaguar

Sleeping in a hammock inside a hut

The Jaguar Shaman, a Tirio Indian from Suriname

listening **Strategy**

Guessing Meaning from Context: Parts of Speech Audio

Sometimes a word can function in different ways. Here are some examples:

He was an <u>apprentice</u> to a shaman.
   (noun = helper/trainee)

He hoped to <u>apprentice</u> himself to a shaman.
   (verb = *become* a helper/trainee)

I don't know what this word <u>means</u>.
   (verb = represents)

This is the only <u>means</u> of reaching my goal.
   (noun = method or way)

A. Recognizing Parts of Speech. `Audio` Listen to each word in the context of two sentences.
Figure out the part of speech and meaning in sentences *a* and *b*. You'll hear each sentence two times.

Word	Part of Speech	Meaning

1. chants   *a.* _____   _____

          b. _____   _____

2. scowl   *a.* _____   _____

        b. _____   _____

        (In this context, *fixed* means "to direct a look at.")

3. alien   *a.* _____   _____

       b. _____   _____

B. Listening for the Main Idea. `Audio` The radio passage you'll hear is part of a program called
Fresh Air. In it, Marti Moss-Coane interviews ethnobotanist Mark Plotkin about his studies among tribal
people in South America. As you listen to the interview the first time, try to answer this question:

• What caused the Jaguar Shaman to change his mind and accept Plotkin as his apprentice?

C. Listening for Details. `Audio` Listen again to the first part of the interview. Listen for the
answers to the following question and write those answers on the lines. (Hint: Listen especially for verbs
and verb phrases.)

• What six steps did a person have to go through in order to become a shaman among the Tirio
Indians?

1. _____

2. _____

3. _____

4. _____

5. _____

6. _____

D. Listening for Reasons. **Audio** Listen again to four short parts of the interview. Write your answers to the questions; write just phrases, not complete sentences. You'll hear each part two times.

1. Why was Plotkin's relationship with the Jaguar Shaman an enigmatic (mysterious) one in the beginning?

   _____

2. Why did the Jaguar Shaman resent Plotkin?

   _____

3. What did the shaman appreciate?

   _____

4. Why might the jaguar be the symbol of the shaman?

   _____

E. Listening for Explanations. **Audio** Plotkin has said that he had an "incredibly vivid dream" of a jaguar. The shaman said that he (the shaman) was the jaguar. Plotkin offers four possible explanations for this experience. What are they? Listen again to one last part of the interview and write your answers.

Possible reasons for the experience

1. _____

2. _____

3. _____

4. _____

After Listening

A. Discussion. **Group** Discuss the answers to these questions.

1. Have you ever had a dream so vivid that you thought it was real? If so, tell your group about it. What do you think it meant?

2. Is there a person in your life (friend, teacher, neighbor, co-worker, etc.) with whom you had a bad beginning but with whom you now have a very good relationship? If so, what finally broke the ice and made it possible for you to like each other?

3. Mark Plotkin says: "I think . . . that these separate realities *do* exist . . . and when you realize that these people know things you don't, that these people can teach you things you can't learn in a classroom, . . . it creates the means to communicate on other planes [= levels of reality]." What's one example from the radio interview of separate realities? What do you think about "separate realities"? Is it possible for separate realities to exist? If so, can you think of an example from your own life, someone else's life, or something that you've read?

B. (Optional) Applying Your Knowledge.   If you have a VCR and access to a video rental store, rent the movie *The Emerald Forest.* Notice in it examples of Amazonian shamanism. With your knowledge of Mark Plotkin's experience, how can you explain the symbols and rituals in the film?

. . : : : : : **Part Five** Academic English: Shamanism

Before Listening

listening Strategy

Preparing to Listen to a Lecture

Most college lectures are fifty minutes long. In their lectures, professors cover information that is different from that in the reading homework, although they may refer to the reading done at home. *The more knowledge you have of the subject before going to a lecture, the more you will understand of the lecture.* The professor will sometimes confirm your knowledge (say what you already know) and sometimes correct it but will most often add to your knowledge.

A. Brainstorming. **Group**   In Parts One, Two, and Four, you learned something about shamanism. Now bring together all of your knowledge of shamans and write it in the blanks. (For example, what are shamans? In what parts of the world can you find shamans? How does one become a shaman? What do shamans do?)

_____

_____

_____

_____

_____

_____

listening Strategy

Having Questions in Mind

It always helps to have questions in mind as you listen. This way, you will be listening for answers to your questions, and you will be a more active listener.

B. Thinking Ahead.

1. Look over the pictures and the partial outline on pages 25–27 for the lecture on shamanism. What questions do you expect (or want) the speaker to answer? Is there anything that you're curious about? Write your questions in the blanks.

_____

_____

_____

_____

2. Now look over the questions in Using Your Notes on pages 28–29. Are any of these similar to your own questions?

C. Guessing Meaning from Context.   In the lecture, you are going to hear some words that may be new to you. Before you listen, guess the meanings of some of the words from the lecture. The words are underlined in the sentences. Look for clues to their meanings in the words around them.

Write your guess in the blank after each sentence. Then check your guess with your teacher or the dictionary.

1. The main goddess in that religion has a <u>dual nature</u>. She's considered to be the goddess of both love and war, so she's gentle and loving, but she's also violent and cruel.

   Guess: (dual) _____

   Guess: (nature) _____

2. I borrowed his CD, and then I lost it a few days later. I feel terrible about it. To <u>make amends</u>, I want to buy him another CD.

   Guess: _____

3. That actor has a lot of <u>charisma</u>. Everyone just *loves* him, and he attracts friends everywhere.

   Guess: _____

4. The magician <u>transformed</u> the silk scarf into a white bird.

Guess: _____

5. In British pubs, people often play a game of <u>darts</u>. The person who throws a dart closest to the center of the target is the winner.

Guess: _____

6. The poor boy knew that his dream of going to medical school was as <u>unattainable</u> as walking on the moon.

Guess: _____

7. The shaman doesn't cure people simply out of kindness. It's his full-time <u>livelihood</u>.

Guess: _____

8. In the movie *The Exorcist,* a little girl's mind and body are completely <u>possessed</u> by an evil spirit.

Guess: _____

9. The <u>spectators</u> in their seats were as excited as the players on the field.

Guess: _____

10. She's not expressing her own ideas. She's just a <u>mouthpiece</u> for the government.

Guess: _____

11. When they heard the voices of their dead ancestors there in the room, the people believed that the shaman had <u>conjured up</u> their ancestors' spirits.

Guess: _____

12. As it was leaving the station, the train was very loud, but as it moved away, the sound became <u>fainter</u> and fainter.

Guess: _____

listening Strategy

Taking Lecture Notes

It's important to take careful notes as you listen to a lecture because exam questions come not only from reading but also from lectures. You'll practice lecture note taking in every chapter of this book. Here are a few general suggestions:

- Don't "just listen" and not take notes at all. You won't remember the information in several weeks, at exam time, and there won't be anything you can study.

- Don't try to write everything. Note taking is not dictation!

- Don't write complete sentences. There probably won't be time.

- In your notes, try to distinguish general from specific points. One way to do this is to keep general points on the left. Indent a little to the right for more specific points. Indent further to the right for small details. A formal outline (as you see on pages 25–27) is one way to do this.

- Use abbreviations whenever possible.

- Predict which words will appear often in a lecture and decide on your *own* abbreviations for them.

D. Using Abbreviations.   The following box contains some common abbreviations that students use. After the box is a list of words that you'll hear often in the lecture. Decide on your own abbreviations for each one.

Common Abbreviations			
about	*abt*	somebody	*sbdy*
and	*+ or &*	something	*sthg*
especially	*esp*	typical/typically	*typ*
essential	*ess*	with	*w/*
important	*imp*	without	*w/out*
means	*=*		

Words in the Lecture   **My Abbreviations**

1. shaman   _____

2. shamanism   _____

3. spirit   _____

Words in the Lecture	My Abbreviations
4. North America	_____
5. South America	_____
6. North American Indians	_____
7. psychology/psychologically	_____
8. transformed	_____
9. hallucinogenic	_____
10. patient (meaning a person)	_____
11. difficult	_____
12. ventriloquist*	_____

*Don't worry about this word. You'll probably be able to guess the meaning when you hear it in the lecture.

Listening

A. Vocabulary: Health and Healing. (Audio)
Listen to the following words and terms in the context of sentences. Each one has a meaning in the list on the right. Write the letter of the meaning next to the word or term it matches.

Words/Terms

Meanings

_____ **1.** at death's door

a. caused by drugs

_____ **2.** ailing

b. almost dead

_____ **3.** afflicted with

c. suffering from

_____ **4.** suck

d. person who works in a profession, especially medicine

_____ **5.** drug-induced

e. sick

_____ **6.** consumption

f. eating or drinking

_____ **7.** invalid

g. take into the mouth by using just the muscles of the mouth

_____ **8.** practitioner

h. person weakened by illness

B. Listening for the Main Idea. (Audio)
You'll hear a lecture called "Shamanism," written by an anthropology professor. Listen once to the entire lecture. (You'll listen again later.) As you listen this time, don't take notes. Instead, follow along with the outline and keep this question in mind:

• What are shamans, and how do they work?

C. Taking Notes. Audio   Listen to the entire lecture again. This time fill in the outline.

Shamanism

Seventeenth century engraving of a shaman

I. What Are Shamans?

   A. The meaning of the word: _____ one who is excited or moved _____

   _____

   B. Where shamanism is found: _____ Korea & NA: _____
   _____ NA S.A. Asia (Korea) _____

   C. Who are shamans? _____ hilers _____ human being / spirit → male / female
   _____ Healers, curers // dual nature _____

II. Shamans, The Individual, And The Community

   A. Why shamans are useful: _____
   _____ Make situation right _____

B. How does a person become a shaman?

    1. Distinctive characteristics of shamans

        a. _character charizma_

        b. _ability to entrance to trans trances—state to communicate_

        c. _ability to id w/ psychology_

    2. Transformation into a shaman: _____

        _____

        _____

C. Some shamanic strategies

    1. Drugs and spirits (Example: Jivaro Indians): _____

        _____

        _____

    2. Shamanistic psychology: _____

        _____

    3. Shamanistic social awareness

        a. _____

        b. _____

III. Chukchee Shamans

A. The trance

    1. How a shaman enters a trance: _____

        _____

Siberian shaman with a drum

2. The spectators: _____

_____

3. Reason for the strange noises made by the shaman: _____

_____

B. "Voices" of the Spirits: The shaman, a talented ventriloquist, can

1. _____

2. _____

3. _____

D. Important Details.   Before doing the next listening exercise, answer as many of these questions as you can, either from memory or from your notes. (The questions are in the same order in which the answers are given in the lecture.) Don't worry yet about the ones you can't answer; you'll have another chance to listen.

1. What function do shamans perform? _____

_____

_____

2. What is the most essential feature of shamanism? Why? _____

_____

_____

3. In societies that believe in shamanism, what do people believe is the cause of misfortune such as disease?

_____

_____

4. What kind of experience does a person usually have to undergo before becoming a shaman?

_____

_____

5. In what kind of case does a shaman most often succeed? _____

_____

_____

6. Typically, what happens when a shaman enters a trance? What happens when the shaman "returns" from (comes out of) the trance?

_____

_____

_____

7. Among the Chukchee people of Siberia, the shaman enters a trance through the constant beating of a drum. In the trance, he makes a strange noise and "shouts hysterically." What do these sounds mean to the spectators?

_____

_____

8. Waldemar Bogoras describes the trance—and possession by spirits—of a Chukchee shaman who is a talented ventriloquist. From the context (not a dictionary), what do you think a ventriloquist can do?

_____

_____

E. Listening Again for Important Details. (Audio)   Go back to the beginning of Exercise D. Listen again to the parts of the lecture that answer the eight questions. Either check your answers or fill in missing answers.

F. (Optional) Filling in the Gaps. (Audio)   If necessary, listen one last time to the entire lecture and fill in any gaps (missing information) in your outline.

After Listening

A. Using Your Notes.   Use your notes to write your answers to these questions about the lecture. When you finish, compare your answers with a partner's.

1. What is a synonym for the word *shaman?* _____

2. Where is shamanism found today? _____

_____

3. What are some personal characteristics of a successful shaman? _____

_____

4. What are two means by which a shaman can enter a trance? (Ex. Jivaro and Chukchee.)

_____

5. What do people believe is happening to the shaman when he or she is in a trance?

_____

B. Discussion. **Pair** Discuss anything from the lecture that surprised you or interested you. Then make a list of everything that you've learned about shamanism. (Try not to look back at your lecture notes.)

Step Beyond

academic Strategy

Psyching out Your Professors

Students need to be able to predict what kinds of questions their professors will ask on an exam. Making such predictions (a skill that students call "psyching out" the professors) can guide how and what you study. (You saw an example of this in the conversation in Part Two of this chapter.) Here are some suggestions:

- Pay attention to what your professor *emphasizes, repeats, writes on the board,* or *appears to get excited about.*
- Don't be shy about asking your professor or teaching assistant what kinds of questions to expect.
- Consider what kinds of questions appeared on previous exams (if any) in the class.

Practice. With a partner, write three questions that you might expect on an exam about the lecture "Shamanism."

A. Extension.   Ethnobotanist Mark Plotkin once injured his elbow when he was studying plants in the jungles of South America. Partly to find relief for his elbow and partly to learn more about the methods of shamans, he underwent a shaman's healing ritual. Here is his account of that ritual. As you read it, don't worry about new words. Instead, simply pay attention to the steps in the ritual. With a felt-tip pen, mark anything that is familiar to you from the lecture. Also, mark anything that interests you.

A Shaman's Healing Ritual

Night was falling, and the last shafts of sunlight filtered through the forest canopy and into the shelter. The shaman rolled a dry leaf of tobacco into a cylinder and placed it in a pipe made from the brown, woody, cylindrical fruit of the *po-no* tree, a relative of the Brazil nut. He then sprinkled several crushed
5   herbs on top of the tobacco. Striking a match from a box I had given him earlier, he began to smoke the tobacco mixture as he sat down beside me. The musty smell of tobacco mixed with the sweet-smelling aromatic herbs filled the small shelter. With his right hand, he gently shut my eyes and then started to intone a series of chants in order to invoke the spirits (according to the explanation Boss later provided). A
10   period of quiet then ensued as he awaited the arrival of the powers he had summoned. After a while, I heard one of the walls of the hut begin to shake violently as if something or someone were passing through. Then the shaman moaned and began a dialogue between himself and a being that seemed to be speaking through him. This continued for what seemed like hours. I slowly drifted into a dreamlike trance,
15   feeling as if I were sinking deeper and deeper into an enormous featherbed. Suddenly the wall shook again as if our visitor had departed. Silence enveloped us; then I heard the sound of a match being struck and the shaman relit his pipe. He gently took hold of my left wrist and raised my arm, then blew the magical smoke onto my elbow and massaged the area with his thumb. This was repeated three times and then he rubbed
20   the area once more with the cotton swab.

The old medicine man began chanting again, and I felt my body drifting farther downward, like a dry leaf caught in the autumn wind. Down I sank until I felt myself come to rest on a gentle bed of moss. Then I floated up to the top of the hut; from there, I looked down and saw the shaman blowing tobacco smoke over my prone body.
25   The shaman resumed his chanting and I felt myself drifting back down to the floor of the hut. The next thing I remember was him waking me gently by tapping me on the cheek with his fingers. He helped me to my feet; I felt a bit dazed and

rather unsteady. The Wayana led me down the path toward the village by the light of a full moon, which gave the jungle an eerie iridescent silver glow.

30   "Wait here!" commanded the medicine man as he stepped off the path. In a moment he returned, his right fist in a ball. Slowly he uncurled his fingers to reveal three small, sharp, pointed sticks.

"*Yolok peleu,*" he said. "The arrows of the evil spirits." He closed his fist and opened it again. There was nothing there. I was too frightened to ask any questions.

Source: Mark J. Plotkin, Ph.D., excerpts from *Tales of a Shaman's Apprentice.* Copyright © 1993 by Mark J. Plotkin. Reprinted with the permission of Viking Penguin, a division of Penguin Putnam Inc.

speaking Strategy

Synthesizing Information

One common type of question on essay exams is a **synthesis** question. In other words, the professor requires you to *put together* information from different sources—from the class lectures and the reading. If you study in a small group of classmates, you can share your ideas and learn from each other.

Example: A: Remember how Dr. Hicks mentioned the use of drugs to cause a vision during the ritual?

B: Yeah. I've got that somewhere in my notes.

C: Yeah! That's right. And Plotkin says the healer smoked tobacco and herbs. Do you think there was something hallucinogenic in that tobacco?

B. Synthesizing Information. **Group**   Analyze Plotkin's description of the healing ritual. Find at least four elements of the ritual that are familiar to you from the lecture. Work together to answer (orally) this question. Present your findings to the class.

- How would an anthropologist explain this ritual? What elements are typical of shamanic healing rituals?

C. Discussion. **Group**   Discuss the answers to these questions.

1. What are the functions of a belief in spirits and shamans? In other words, why do many societies believe in the power of spirits and shamans?

2. What apparently "irrational" beliefs exist in modern urban societies, and what purpose do these beliefs serve?

chapter Two

Physical Anthropology

Physical anthropology
is the study of the
development of humans.
In this chapter, you'll
listen to information
about and discuss
similarities and
differences among
primates—both human
and nonhuman.

. . : : ! ! **Part One** Introduction: A Window into the Mind of an Ape

Rex Harrison talking with animals in the movie *Doctor Dolittle*

A. Thinking Ahead. **Pair**   Briefly discuss the answers to these questions.

1. Do animals communicate? How? What kinds of messages do animals communicate to each other? Give some examples.

2. How do you think chimpanzees or gorillas communicate with each other in the wild? In other words, what kinds of communication do they use?

3. If you need an English word that you don't know, do you sometimes create a new word? If so, can you think of words that you have created? Did people understand you?

B. Reading. Read this excerpt from a chapter in an anthropology textbook.

Apes and Sign Language

Experiments have shown that apes can learn to use, if not speak, true language (Miles 1983). Several apes have learned to converse with people through means other than speech. One such communication system is American Sign Language, or Ameslan, which is widely used by deaf and mute Americans. Ameslan employs a limited
5 number of basic gesture units that are analogous to sounds in spoken language. These units combine to form words and larger units of meaning.

The chimpanzee Nim, in a photo taken by Susan Kuklin, makes the sign for "me."

The first chimpanzee to learn Ameslan was Washoe, a female. . . . Washoe lived in a trailer and heard no spoken language. The researchers always used Ameslan to communicate with each other in her presence. The chimp gradually acquired an expressive vocabu-
10 lary of 132 signs representing English words (Gardner, Gardner, and Van Cantfort 1989). At the age of two, Washoe began to combine as many as five signs into rudimentary sentences such as "you, me, go out, hurry." . . . Work with other chimps, along with Washoe's later progress, showed that apes can distinguish between subject and object.

The second chimp to learn Ameslan was Lucy, Washoe's junior by one year. . . . From
15 her second day of life . . . Lucy lived with a family in Norman, Oklahoma. Roger Fouts, a researcher from the nearby Institute for Primate Studies, came two days a week to test and improve Lucy's knowledge of Ameslan. During the rest of the week, Lucy used Ameslan to converse with her foster parents. After acquiring language, Washoe and Lucy expressed

several human traits: swearing, joking, telling lies, and trying to teach language to others.
20 . . . Both Washoe and Lucy have tried to teach Ameslan to other animals, including their
own offspring. . . .

Gorilla Koko and human Penny Patterson

Because of their size and strength as adults, gorillas are less likely subjects than chimps
for such experiments. Lean adult male gorillas in the wild weigh 400 pounds (180 kilograms), and full-grown females can easily reach 250 pounds (110 kilograms). Because of
25 this, psychologist Penny Patterson's work with gorillas at Stanford University seems more
daring than the chimp experiments. Patterson raised her now full-grown female gorilla,
Koko, in a trailer next to a Stanford museum. Koko's vocabulary surpasses that of any
chimp. She regularly employs 400 Ameslan signs and
has used about 700 at least once. Asking, in the evening,
30 to get into her bedroom, Koko gestures "Penny, open key
hurry bedroom." What she is saying, translated into
English, is "Penny, unlock my bedroom door and be quick
about it."

Koko and the chimps also show that apes share still
35 another linguistic ability with humans—productivity.
Speakers routinely use the rules of their language to produce entirely new expressions that are comprehensible
to other native speakers. I can, for example, create
"baboonlet" to refer to a baboon infant. I do this by anal-
40 ogy with English words in which the suffix -let desig-
nates the young of a species. Anyone who speaks English

Baby baboon

immediately understands the meaning of my new word. Koko, Washoe, and Lucy have shown that apes also use language productively. Lucy used gestures
45 she already knew to create "drinkfruit" for watermelon. Washoe, seeing a swan for the first time, coined "waterbird." Koko, who knew the gestures for "finger" and "bracelet," formed "finger bracelet" when she was given a ring. Similarly, she called a
50 mask an "eye hat." . . .

Swan swimming

No one denies the huge difference between human language and gorilla signs. There is a major gap between the ability to write a book or say a prayer and the few hundred gestures employed by a well-
55 trained chimp. Apes aren't people, but they aren't just animals either. Let Koko express it: When asked by a reporter whether she was a person or an animal, Koko chose neither. Instead, she signed "fine animal gorilla" (Patterson 1978).

C. Vocabulary Check. Find words in the reading passage that mean the following:

First paragraph:

people who can't hear = _____

uses (verb) = _____

Second paragraph:

primitive, basic, simple = _____

Third paragraph:

saying vulgar ("bad") words = _____

Fourth paragraph:

goes beyond; is better than = _____

Fifth paragraph:

baby = _____

comparison = _____

created or made up (a word) = _____

Sixth paragraph:

difference = _____

movements of the hands to communicate meaning = _____

newspaper journalist = _____

D. Discussion. (Group)   Discuss the answers to these questions.

1. In what way do apes (chimps and gorillas) and humans seem to be similar in their use of language? In what ways are they different?

2. What information in the reading did you find interesting?

3. Do you know of other studies of apes and language? If so, tell your group what you know.

E. Freewriting.   Choose *one* of these topics. Write about it for fifteen minutes. Don't worry about grammar and don't use a dictionary. Just put as many ideas as you can on paper.

• your reaction to the textbook reading

• an experience you have had communicating with any kind of nonhuman animal

• questions that you would like to ask an ape who can communicate with you

Part Two Everyday English: Chimps Like Us

Before Listening

A. Thinking Ahead. (Group)   Discuss what you know about **evolution**—the scientific idea that animals (including humans) developed from fewer, simpler animals.

1. Who was Charles Darwin? Can you name other scientists who have contributed to this field?

2. What evidence do we have of evolution?

3. Some religious groups in the United States reject the idea of evolution because it contradicts the Bible. What is your opinion? Is this way of thinking common among any groups in your native country or culture?

B. Vocabulary Preparation: Informal Words.   The students in the conversation that you'll hear use some words and expressions that are commonly found in casual conversation. First, read each sentence and guess the meaning of the underlined words. Then choose their meaning from the definitions in the box. Write the letters in the blanks.

> **Definitions**
>
> *a.* great; wonderful   *d.* stay with
>
> *b.* convenient   *e.* take quickly
>
> *c.* and other, similar things

Sentences

_____ **1.** I'm going to <u>stick with</u> this exercise program even though it's very hard for me.

_____ **2.** Two-year-old children can be like monkeys; they often just <u>grab</u> what they want instead of asking first.

_____ **3.** A shelf above your desk is a <u>handy</u> place to keep your textbooks.

_____ **4.** I enjoy cultural anthropology. I like learning about different belief systems <u>and all</u>.

_____ **5.** I love learning about how animals think and how intelligent they are. I think it's really <u>cool</u>.

Listening

A. Listening for the Main Idea. `Video/Audio`   Listen to the conversation one time. As you listen, try to answer this question:

- According to Jennifer, in what ways are humans and other primates—such as chimpanzees and gorillas—similar?

B. Listening for Details. `Video/Audio`   Listen again to the conversation. Then write your answers to these questions. Write short phrases, not complete sentences.

1. Why is Jennifer going to take physical anthropology?

   _____

2. What do students learn about in a physical anthropology class?

   _____

3. What example does Jennifer give of chimpanzees using tools?

   _____

4. How does Brandon think chimpanzee tool use is different from human tool use?

   _____

5. What is one example of how nonhuman primates use language?

   _____

6. How does Brandon think Koko's use of language is different from a human's use of language?

   _____

C. Listening for Emotions. `Video/Audio`   Sometimes it's important to hear the emotions behind what a person says. You can get extra information this way. Listen again. This time, you are going to hear only parts of the conversation. As you listen, pay attention to the way you think the speaker feels. Circle the feeling that best describes what you hear.

1. How does Jennifer feel about taking physical anthropology?

   a. She's happy about it.

   b. She's unhappy about it.

   c. She doesn't care about it.

2. How does Victor react to what Jennifer says?

    a. He's interested in this information.

    b. He's a little insulted or angry.

    c. He's not interested in the subject.

3. Which statement best explains how Victor's feelings change?

    a. First he feels confident. Then he feels less confident.

    b. First he's angry. Then he's less angry.

    c. First he doesn't feel confident. Then he feels more confident.

4. How does Jennifer feel when she answers Brandon?

    a. She feels unsure of herself.

    b. She feels sure of herself.

    c. She feels confused.

5. Which statement best describes the way that Victor feels?

    a. He is bored.

    b. He wants to talk about a different subject.

    c. He is excited.

After Listening

A. Guessing Meaning from Context.   In the conversation, you heard some new words or terms. Guess the meanings of some of the words from the conversation. The words are underlined in the sentences. Look for clues to their meanings in the words around them.

    Write your guess in the blank after each sentence. Compare your answers with a partner's. Then check your guess with your teacher or the dictionary.

1. We plan ahead. We know we need to accomplish a task, like get food, and we design an <u>implement</u> specifically for that purpose.

    Guess: _____

2. Can this gorilla use sign language to make up original sentences? If so, then I would say that's "language." If not, then it's just <u>imitative behavior</u>.

    Guess: _____

3. Hey, Brandon, it sounds as if you <u>take exception</u> to being compared to a chimpanzee.

    Guess: _____

B. Synthesizing Information. **Pair**   In the conversation, Brandon says: "Can this gorilla use sign language to make up original sentences? If so, then I would say that's 'language.' If not, then it's just imitative behavior." Look again at the reading in Part One on pages 35–37. According to Brandon's definition, are gorillas and chimps capable of using language, or are they using just imitative behavior?

C. Information Gap: How Are They Related? **Pair**   Work with a partner. Together, look over the pictures and information on pages 42–43. Then, to learn how different primates are related to each other, one partner will work on page 44 and the other on page 264. Don't look at your partner's page. Take turns asking and answering questions about primates. Write your answers in the boxes on the primate family tree.

   Ask your partner questions such as these:

- What are the two/three <u>suborders</u> within the <u>order</u> _____?

<u>infraorders</u>	<u>suborder</u>
<u>superfamilies</u>	<u>infraorder</u>
<u>families</u>	<u>superfamily</u>

- How do you spell _____?
- What are examples of _____?
- What are two/three types of _____?

Gibbons
From southeast Asia, gibbons and siamangs (slightly larger than gibbons) are completely arboreal; that is, they live in trees and move around by clinging and swinging from tree to tree.

Orangutans
Native to Indonesia, orangs are usually solitary animals. They typically climb trees but don't often swing from tree to tree.

Spider monkeys
These and other New World monkeys are the only primates with prehensile tails—in other words, tails that can grasp tree branches.

Lemurs
There are at least 23 species of lemurs, all from the island of Madagascar. Some are arboreal and some partially terrestrial.

Chimpanzees
Chimps, terrestrial apes native to Africa, live in communities of about 50 members. They are the closest relative to humans.

Baboons
An Old World monkey, the baboon is terrestrial and lives in a troop (group) that has a dominance hierarchy.

Student A

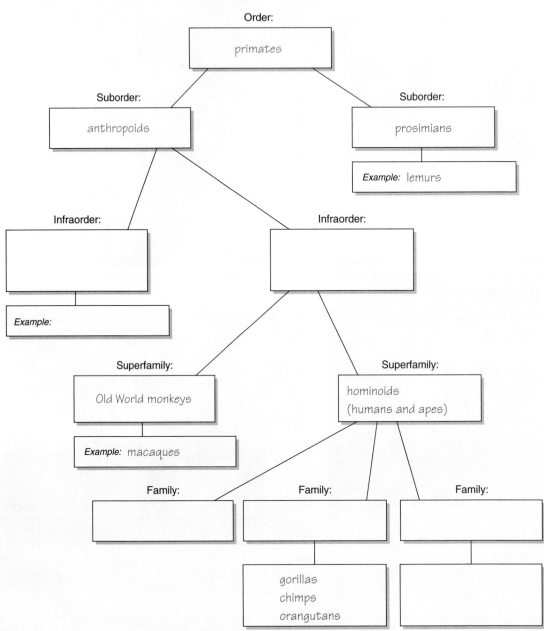

Primate Family Tree

Order:

primates

Suborder:

anthropoids

Suborder:

prosimians

Example: lemurs

Infraorder:

Infraorder:

Example:

Superfamily:

Old World monkeys

Superfamily:

hominoids
(humans and apes)

Example: macaques

Family:

Family:

Family:

gorillas
chimps
orangutans

·.:∴∶ **Part Three** The Mechanics of Listening and Speaking

Language Functions

Expressing an Opinion Audio

Your expression of an opinion can be strong or soft. Here are some examples:

Strong: Dr. Taylor gave a boring lecture today.

Soft: <u>It seems to me that</u> Dr. Taylor's lecture today was really boring.

              <u>I think</u> Dr. Taylor gave a boring lecture today.

              Dr. Taylor gave a boring lecture today, <u>in my opinion</u>.

Notice that adding an opinion expression ("It seems to me," "I think," "In my opinion") softens your statement.

Expressing Agreement or Disagreement Audio

There are many ways to express agreement or disagreement with someone's opinion. Here are some expressions:

Agreement
- I agree. (Note: It's incorrect to say "I'm agree.")
- I agree with that.
- I agree with you.
- I'm with you.

- You're right.
- I couldn't agree more.
- I completely agree.

Disagreement
- I'm not so sure about that.
- I disagree.
- I don't agree.
- I disagree with that.
- I disagree with you.
- I completely disagree.
- You're wrong.

softer

stronger

The first example of disagreement is soft. The next four are neutral—that is, neither soft nor strong. The last two are strong. You can soften disagreement by adding "sorry." Here are some examples:

- <u>Sorry</u>, I don't agree.

- <u>I'm sorry</u>, but I disagree with you.

A. Practice. **Pair**   Express your opinion about the following. Express both strong and soft opinions. Agree or disagree with your partner. Then exchange roles.

What's Your Opinion?

1. Are chimpanzees intelligent?

2. Can animals use tools?

3. Is primate "language" the same as human language?

4. Should we lock wild animals in cages in zoos for human amusement?

5. Should children be taught about evolution in school?

Intonation

Softening Disagreement   **Audio**

In addition to using the word *sorry,* there are other ways to soften disagreement.

1. You can add a few words such as "Wait a minute . . ." (in informal English) or "Well . . ." before disagreeing. Also, notice the vowel length in the following examples.

   Wait a minute. I don't agree with that.

   Well, I'm not so sure about that.

2. To make disagreement even softer, more careful, you can appear at first to agree before adding the word *but.* Here is an example:

   A: Both humans and chimps use tools.

   B: I agree, but I think humans' tool use is more complex.

3. You can also add a tag question. Here is an example:

   A: Both humans and chimps use tools.

   B: I understand what you're saying, but humans' tool use is much more complex, isn't it?

4. Often, your intonation alone—not your words—signals the listener that disagreement will follow. This is perhaps the softest form of disagreement.

   Notice the subtle differences in intonation (especially vowel length) in these examples.

Agreement:	I agree.	**Disagreement:**	I agree, . . .
	I agree with that.		I agree with that, . . .
	I completely agree.		I completely agree, . . .

B. Practice. **Audio**   Listen to these short conversations. Is Speaker B's disagreement soft, neutral, or strong? Listen for the use of expressions such as "sorry," initial agreement followed by the word *but,* a tag question, intonation, and vowel length. Circle your answers.

1.   soft   neutral   strong   4.   soft   neutral   strong

2.   soft   neutral   strong   5.   soft   neutral   strong

3.   soft   neutral   strong   6.   soft   neutral   strong

C. Practice. **Audio**   Listen to Person B's response in the following exchanges. In each case, Person B *says* he/she agrees, but is this true? Listen for Person B's intonation to decide what is actually in this person's mind; in other words, do you expect Person B to add *but* and then disagree? Check (✓) your answers.

	Person B truly agrees.	Person B will probably add *but* and disagree.
1.	_____	_____
2.	_____	_____
3.	_____	_____
4.	_____	_____
5.	_____	_____

Pronunciation

The Voiceless *th* Sound*   **Audio**

The voiceless *th* sounds the same as /t/ to some students and /s/ to others, but these three sounds are pronounced differently. Listen to these contrasts:

t	s	th
tank	sank	thank
tick	sick	thick
team	seem	theme
bet	Bess	Beth
pat	pass	path

These contrasts exist in many ordinal numbers. Here are some examples:

fourth   fifth   sixth   seventh   eighth   ninth   tenth   eleventh   twelfth

Note: The IPA (International Phonetic Alphabet) symbol for this sound is: /θ/

Listen to these contrasts:

t	s	th
for<u>t</u>	for<u>ce</u>	four<u>th</u>
eigh<u>t</u>	a<u>ce</u>	eigh<u>th</u>
ten<u>t</u>	ten<u>se</u>	ten<u>th</u>

D. Practice. **Audio**   In each group of words, circle the one that you hear.

1.	tank	sank	thank	**7.**	team	seem	theme
2.	tin	sin	thin	**8.**	tent	tense	tenth
3.	pat	pass	path	**9.**	eight	ace	eighth
4.	tick	sick	thick	**10.**	mat	mass	math
5.	fort	force	fourth	**11.**	bet	Bess	Beth
6.	tie	sigh	thigh				

E. Practice. **Audio**   Look again at the box on pages 47–48. Repeat the words after the speaker.

F. Practice. **Audio**   Read along as you listen to this short conversation. Then listen again and repeat each sentence after the speaker. Pay special attention to words with *th*.

A: You have an Anthro class on Thursday, don't you?

B: Yeah. Anthro 330.

A: Is that over on North Campus?

B: No. South Campus. It's in Thorne Hall.

Review: Language Functions

Expressing an Opinion and Expressing Disbelief or Disagreement **Video/Audio**

Listen to these examples of how to express opinions and agree and disagree. You'll use these functions in the next section.

Put It Together

Agreeing and Disagreeing

Practice. **Pair**   Work with a partner. Express your opinion about the following. Give both soft and strong opinions. Agree or disagree with your partner. If you disagree, use strong, soft, or neutral disagreement, depending on how you feel. Pay attention to intonation and choice of words to soften disagreement. Remember to pronounce *th* correctly.

Topics

- a course or major you particularly like or dislike
- a music video you like or dislike
- a computer game you like or dislike
- a website you visited recently
- a new TV show
- a movie you saw recently
- zoos
- teaching language to chimps and gorillas

::::: **Part Four** Broadcast English: An Exhibit
at the Copenhagen Zoo

Before Listening

A. Thinking Ahead.   You are going to hear a radio program about an exhibit at the Copenhagen Zoo. Before you listen, try to answer these questions:

1. Which primates do you expect to see at a zoo?

2. What interests zoo visitors about primate exhibits?

B. Vocabulary Preparation.   You are going to hear some new words in the radio program. First, read each sentence and guess the meaning of the underlined words. Then choose their meaning from the definitions in the box. Write the letters in the blanks.

Sentences

_____ **1.** Everyone <u>went ape over</u> the new exhibit. The crowds were so heavy that I couldn't see a thing.

_____ **2.** People have been <u>thronging</u> to the music festival. At last count, over 100,000 tickets had been sold.

_____ **3.** There were so many people in the audience that I couldn't get a <u>glimpse</u> of the stage.

_____ **4.** The animals lived in a <u>plexiglas</u> house so they could stay warm but still be visible to zoo visitors.

_____ **5.** He was a well-known <u>acrobat</u> in the circus until he fell from the high wire and injured his back.

_____ **6.** We will have to wait five years in order to learn about the <u>long-term impact</u> of the new educational programs.

_____ **7.** We received so many <u>queries</u> about the new programs that we couldn't answer them all; instead, we put up an informative website.

_____ **8.** While human fathers take care of their <u>offspring</u>, many nonhuman primate fathers disappear long before the babies are born.

_____ **9.** I didn't want to get up and give my speech to the class because the previous speaker had been wonderful, and that was a <u>hard act to follow</u>.

Definitions
a. questions
b. quick look
c. was very excited about
d. babies
e. made of clear sheets of plastic
f. coming in large crowds
g. very successful performance with which you don't want your own performance compared
h. effect in the far future
i. person with great gymnastic skill

Listening

A. Listening for Main Ideas. (Audio) Listen to the radio interview. As you listen, try to answer these questions:

- Which primates are in this exhibit?
- How do zoo visitors react to them?

B. Listening for Explicit Reasons. (Audio) Listen again to two sentences from the interview. In each sentence, the word *because* introduces a reason. Write short answers to these questions.

1. Why doesn't Henrik perform? _____

_____ (Who are his neighbors?) _____

2. Why hasn't it been necessary to erect a sign warning "Please do not feed the *Homo sapiens*"?

_____

listening Strategy

Listening for Implicit Reasons (Audio)

Speakers don't always state a reason clearly with a word such as *because*. Instead, they simply **imply** (suggest) a reason in the context. You need to be aware of a logical, implicit cause-effect relationship.

C. Listening for Implicit Reasons. (Audio) Listen again to four short parts of the interview. Write your answers to these questions.

1. Why does the Copenhagen Zoo have this exhibit?

_____

2. Why don't zoo visitors spend much time in front of the human cage?

_____

3. Why do the humans' neighbors scream every hour or two?

_____

4. If Henrik and Melina become part of a zoo exhibit in the future, why won't there be just the two of them?

_____

_____

After Listening

A. Discussion. Group   Discuss the answers to these questions.

1. Have you ever been to the primate exhibit at a zoo? If so, which primates did you see? What were they doing? Which primates attracted the most attention from zoo visitors?

2. Do you think that primates might behave differently in a zoo from the way they behave in the wild? If so, why?

B. (Optional) Doing Research.   Go to a public place (shopping mall, park, zoo, etc.) and observe the *Homo sapiens* as if they were a primate species about which you know nothing. Make notes on your observations on the chart on this page. Then share your findings with the class.

Observation	
Place: _____	Date: _____
Diet (what is eaten)	
Use of tools	
Communication (gestures, calls, facial expression, body language, language)	
Method(s) of moving from place to place	
Treatment of offspring	

:·:::: **Part Five** Academic English: Human and Nonhuman Primate Behavior

Before Listening

Jane Goodall and wild chimps in Gombe, Tanzania

A. Brainstorming. **Group**   Bring together your knowledge of primates and primate behavior by answering these questions. Write your answers in the blanks.

1. What are some nonhuman primates? List them.

_____   _____

_____   _____

_____   _____

_____   _____

2. Brainstorm everything that you already know or believe about the following:

• How primates move from place to place:

_____   _____

_____   _____

_____   _____

- What primates eat:

  _____   _____

  _____   _____

- Which primates use tools and how they do this:

  _____

  _____

- How primates care for their young:

  _____

  _____

B. Pre-Test.   Before you listen to the lecture, see how much you already know about the behavior of humans and nonhuman primates. Answer these questions. Don't worry about being right or wrong. You'll learn the answers in the lecture.

1. Humans, apes, monkeys, and prosimians are all primates.   True or false? _____

2. Humans, apes, monkeys, and prosimians share a common ancestor who lived approximately 65 million years ago.   True or false? _____

3. Humans and monkeys share a common ancestor who lived approximately 25 million years ago.   True or false? _____

4. How do baboons move around their environment most of the time?

   a. by swinging through the trees

   b. by walking on the ground on four **limbs** (arms/legs)

   c. by walking in the trees on four limbs

   d. by walking on the ground on four limbs but with the weight of the front limbs on the knuckles instead of the flat hands

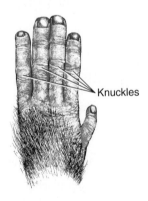
Knuckles

5. How do chimps and gorillas move around their environment most of the time?

  a. by swinging through the trees

  b. by walking on the ground on four limbs

  c. by walking in the trees on four limbs

  d. by walking on the ground on four limbs but with the weight of the front limbs on the knuckles instead of the flat hands

6. According to fossil evidence, which probably happened first?

  a. Our early human ancestors began to use and carry tools.

  b. Our early human ancestors began to walk on two feet.

7. Two early species of humans (which don't exist today) are *Homo habilis* and *Homo erectus*.   True or false? _____

8. In general, primates provide more parental care to their offspring than most other mammals.   True or false? _____

9. Humans differ from nonhuman primates in that

  a. only humans provide for their offspring after the young are **weaned** from mother's milk

  b. the human father provides much of the care for the offspring, but the nonhuman primate father rarely does

  c. the death rate in young humans is lower than in nonhuman primates

  d. all of the above

10. Which is true about primate diet?

  a. Humans hunt for and eat meat.

  b. Chimpanzees hunt for and eat meat.

  c. Gorillas hunt for and eat meat.

  d. Both *a* and *b*.

  e. Both *a* and *c*.

C. Vocabulary Preparation: Stems and Affixes. **Pair**   Parts of words, usually from Greek or Latin, will help you guess the meaning of many new words. In academic English, and especially in scientific language, there is heavy use of prefixes (the beginning of words), stems (the main part of words), and suffixes (the ending of words). One word that means both prefixes and suffixes is *affixes*. Here are some from the lecture. Can you think of any examples of words with these stems and affixes? If so, write them in the blanks. Then guess the meaning of the underlined words in the sentences that follow.

Prefixes	Meanings	Examples
bi	two	_____
quadr	four	_____
Stems		
arbor	tree	_____
habil	able, capable	_____
homo	human	_____
loco	place	_____
mort	death	_____
motor	move	_____
pater	father	_____
ped	foot	_____
terr	land, earth	_____

1. An example of a terrestrial <u>quadruped</u> is the baboon.

   Guess: _____

2. The <u>locomotor</u> style of humans is referred to as <u>bipedalism</u>.

   Guess: (locomotor) _____

   Guess: (bipedalism) _____

3. The human ancestor that first used tools was *Homo habilis*.

   Guess: _____

4. Young animals that have a large amount of parental care usually have a lower <u>mortality</u> rate.

Guess: _____

5. <u>Paternal</u> care involves provisioning (providing food), protection from predators, and infant transportation.

Guess: _____

D. Using Abbreviations.
The following box contains some common abbreviations that students use when they take lecture notes. After the box is a list of words that you'll hear often in the lecture. Decide on your own abbreviation for each one.

Common Abbreviations			
approximately	approx/≈	relative	rel
depend/dependent	dep	similar/similarity	sim
different/difference	dif	unusual	unus
distinct/distinction	dist	usual	usu
hypothesis	hyp	year(s)	yr(s)
identity	ident	million	mill

Words in the Lecture   **My Abbreviations**

1. behavior   _____

2. human(s)   _____

3. nonhuman primate(s)   _____

4. primate(s)   _____

5. ancestor(s)   _____

6. chimpanzee   _____

7. *Homo habilis*   _____

8. *Homo erectus*   _____

9. environment   _____

10. termites   _____

academic Strategy

Using Abbreviations

Some of the words for which you'll use abbreviations (such as the ones in the boxes on pages 23 and 57) are very common, and you can hear them in any class lecture. Others may be specific to a certain field, such as physical anthropology. Others are *so* specific that you might hear them frequently in only one lecture—such as one on nonhuman primate behavior.

It's a good idea to put a key to your own abbreviations at the top of the page on which you take notes. By doing this, you'll be able to understand your own notes several weeks in the future, as you're studying for an exam, when you might have forgotten what was in your mind on the day of the lecture.

Practice.   As you listen to the lecture, find other words different from the ones in Exercise D and provide your own abbreviations. After the lecture, compare them with a partner's.

Listening

A. Vocabulary: Words in Physical Anthropology. (Audio)   Listen to the following words and terms in the context of sentences. Each one has a meaning in the list on the right. Write the letter of the meaning next to the word or term it matches.

Words/Terms

_____ **1.** fossils

_____ **2.** hypothesis (plural = hypotheses)

_____ **3.** primatologist

_____ **4.** predator

_____ **5.** hand axes

_____ **6.** crude choppers

_____ **7.** propose

Meanings

a. animal that hunts another animal

b. suggest

c. something that now remains of a plant or animal from past geological times

d. person who studies humans, apes, monkeys, and prosimians

e. theory

f. See the pictures on page 59.

g. See the pictures on page 59.

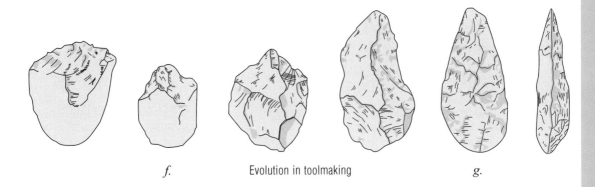

f.   Evolution in toolmaking   *g.*

listening Strategy

Taking Lecture Notes (Audio)

If you know that in the lecture your professor is going to contrast two areas, you might organize your notes differently from the way you organize a formal outline.

Put a vertical line down the center of your page. Divide one topic from the next by drawing a horizontal line.

B. Listening for Main Ideas. (Audio) You'll hear a lecture called "Human and Nonhuman Primate Behavior," written by a physical anthropology professor. Listen once to the entire lecture. As you listen, follow along with the partial notes on pages 60–61. This time, write *only* the four main topics that the speaker covers (A, B, C, and D) and notice any words that you might want to abbreviate. You'll listen again later and fill in details. As you listen, try to answer this question:

- What four behavior patterns of humans and nonhuman primates does the speaker compare?

My Abbreviations: Key

Human and Nonhuman Primate Behavior

Intro.:

1. _Humans, apes, monkeys and prosimians_ _____ —all primates

2. all 4 share a common ancestor _____

3. _____ approx. 25 mill. yrs ago

Humans

A. _____

    _____ = walking

    on the 2 hind limbs

    earliest evidence:

    _____

    _____

    earliest stone tools:

    _____

    one hypothesis:

    _____

    _____

    _____

B. _____

    1. Oldowan tool trad. =

    _____

    _____

      a. remained unchanged

        for _____ yrs

      b. created by

      _____

    2. new type of tool =

    _____

      a. were used until

      _____

Nonhuman Primates

1. _____

2. _____

    a. _____

    b. caupchin monkeys

    c. baboon

3. knuckle-walking

    a. _____

    b. _____

1. Jane Goodall observed

    _____

    _____

    _____

    _____

    _____

2. Another primatologist found

    _____

    _____

  b. used for   However, tool use is

  _____   _____

  _____   _____

  _____   _____

  c. created by

  _____

3. Tool use by hum. ancestors involved:

  a. _____

  b. _____

  c. _____

  (not found among nonhum.

  primates)

C. _____

  1. Sim.: Both _____ & _____

  are _____

  But _____   1. Must _____

  _____   _____

  2. Dif.: _____   2. _____

  _____   _____

  a. provisioning

  b. _____

  c. _____

  d. result: _____

  _____

D. _____

  much food provided by father =   1. diet rarely has _____

  _____   2. exception: _____

                                                       _____

                                                       _____

C. Taking Notes. (Audio)   Listen to the entire lecture again. This time, complete your notes with the important details.

D. Using Your Notes.   Answer as many of these questions as you can, either from memory or from your notes. Don't worry yet about the ones that you can't answer; you'll have another chance to listen. Work alone.

1. What are four primates? _____

2. When did they all share a common ancestor? _____

3. According to fossil, behavioral, and molecular data, what happened approximately 25 million

   years ago? _____

   _____

4. What are four primate locomotor patterns? _____

   _____

5. Approximately, how long ago did the first bipedal human walk? _____

   _____

6. Why did early humans become bipedal? _____

   _____

   _____

7. How long ago were the first stone tools used? _____

8. What species of humans created a more advanced stone tool? _____ Until

   approximately when were these used? _____

9. What is an example of a nonhuman primate that uses tools, and what are two tools that it

   uses? _____

   _____

10. What is the main difference between humans and nonhuman primates in their use of tools?

_____

11. What are two differences between humans' and nonhuman primates' parenting? _____

_____

_____

12. What is the only primate (besides humans) that hunts for meat? _____

_____

E. Listening for Specific Information. (Audio) Listen again to the entire lecture. This time, listen specifically for the answers to any questions that you left blank in Exercise D.

After Listening

A. Post-Test. (Pair) Go back to the pre-test on pages 54–55. Are there some answers that you now need to change?

B. Discussion. (Group) Discuss anything from the lecture that surprised you or interested you. Then make a list of everything that you've learned about primates. (Try not to look back at your notes.) When you finish, write three questions that you might expect to see on an exam about the lecture. Compare your exam questions with those of other groups.

 *Step* Beyond

A. Choosing a Topic. Choose *one* of the following projects to do either by yourself or in a small group.

Project 1

If you have access to a VCR and a video rental store, rent either the film *Gorillas in the Mist* or *Planet of the Apes*. As you watch the film, take notes. Focus especially on the answers to these questions:

• What nonhuman primate behavior do you notice in the film that was mentioned in this chapter?

• What can you learn (from *Gorillas in the Mist*) about the behavior of gorillas in the wild?

Project 2

If you live near a zoo or wild animal park, spend an hour there observing nonhuman primates—lemurs, monkeys, gibbons, orangutans, gorillas, or chimps. As you watch them, take notes. Focus especially on the answers to these questions:

- What nonhuman primate behavior do you notice that was mentioned in this chapter?

- What behavior is similar to human behavior? What behavior is different?

Project 3

Choose *one* nonhuman primate—lemurs, monkeys, gibbons, orangutans, gorillas, or chimpanzees. Do some Web or library research on this primate and learn as much about it as you can. Take notes on what you learn.

B. Reporting Your Information. Class   Organize your notes. Then give a brief report (3–5 minutes) to the class on what you have learned.

Literature

chapter Three

Poetry

In this chapter, you'll read and discuss a number of poems. You'll listen to a somewhat shocking radio interview with a well-known American poet, and you'll hear a lecture explaining three impulses in American poetry.

. . : : : : : **Part One** Introduction to Poetry

A. Thinking Ahead. **Pair**   Before reading the three poems in this section, try to answer these questions:

1. Do you read poetry for pleasure? Did you read it in school? If so, who are your favorite poets? What are your favorite themes in poetry?

2. What are some differences between **contemporary** (modern) poetry and poetry from the past?

3. What can be expressed better in poetry than in fiction or nonfiction?

B. Reading. **Audio**   As you read these three contemporary poems, simply try to enjoy the poems and to get the main idea of each. You can also listen to them and follow along.

Gypsies
by Alden Nowlan

Jessie, my cousin, remembers there were gypsies

every spring, cat-eyes in smoky faces,

hair like black butter on leather laces.

Mothers on the high waggons whose babes sucked

5 flesh on O'Brien Street, I'd be ashamed.

The men stole everything and damned if they didn't

shrug if you caught them—giving back a hen

filched from your own coop like a gift to a peasant.

The little girls danced, their red skirts winking,

10 their legs were lovely, greasy as drumsticks.

And they kidnapped children. Oh, every child

hoped secretly to be stolen by gypsies.

> **shrug** = move the shoulders to mean "I don't care"
> **filched** = stolen
> **coop** = house for chickens

Source: Alden Nowlan, "Gypsies" from *Playing the Jesus Game: Selected Poems* (Trumansburg, N.Y., New/Books, 1977). Reprinted with the permission of Mrs. Claudine Nowlan.

You Understand the Requirements

by Lyn Lifshin

We are
sorry to have to
regret to
tell you
5 sorry sorry
regret sorry that you have
failed

your hair should have been
piled up higher

10 you have failed to
pass failed
your sorry
regret your
final hair comprehensive
15 exam satisfactorily
you understand the requirements

> **comprehensive** = an exam that includes everything in a course

you understand we are
sorry final

and didn't look as professional
20 as desirable
or sorry dignified
and have little enough
sympathy for 16th century
sorry english anglicanism

> **doctoral** = Ph.D.

25 we don't know doctoral
competency what to think and
regret you will sorry not
be able to stay
or finish

30 final regret your disappointment
the unsuccessfully completed best
wishes for the future
it has been a
regret sorry the requirements
35 the university policy
       please don't call us.

Thinking Twice in the Laundromat

by Harley Elliott

1. *Bird Dance*

Seeing you
in the laundromat
a beautiful African
5 form   certain and terse
as dark wood

I began my little
bird dance of hope
    afraid I may say something
10   small town and inane
            like
      "welcome to america"

small town (adj.) = unsophisticated
inane = stupid; foolish

Your arm
loading clothes in an arc
15   into the shining chrome circle
is alive

    as something that should
    point over plains
        (the other hand shading
20   your eyes)
I am there
among mimosa trees

plains = wide spaces of flat land

I release green birds toward you
I approach you
25   and my arms are full of long
    rare feathers

I will buy you soap

    I will help you fold

your gleaming sheets.

30 *2. Pink Blues*

Shyly   after you left
coasting on the memory of your
deep skin
    I found the brown wool sock
35   sprawled outside your dryer

In my hand

knowing the foot it holds
more than I should
    exploring him   (he is
40 solemn he
wears glasses)

and remembering your pink lips

and my pink lips

perhaps it could be
45 someday   the way I'd like
seeing you in a supermarket
I would want
to say
    meet me in the laundromat
50   I have your
    husbands sock
O la, o la.

solemn = very serious

Source: Harley Elliott, "Thinking Twice in the Laundromat" from *Hanging Loose* #8. Reprinted with the permission of the author.

C. Main Ideas.   Identify the theme of each poem. Write the letters in the blanks.

_____ 1. "Gypsies"   *a.* a feeling of not succeeding

_____ 2. "You Understand the Requirements"   *b.* a stereotype of a group of people
                                                         whom one hasn't met
_____ 3. "Thinking Twice in the Laundromat"
                                                     c. a man's fascination with a
                                                         beautiful woman

D. Discussion.   **Group**   Briefly discuss each poem by answering these questions.

"Gypsies"

1. From whom did the poet learn about gypsies?

2. What are some of the stereotypes of gypsies in this poem? According to the poem, what two crimes did gypsies commit?

3. What did children hope secretly for?

"You Understand the Requirements"

4. There seem to be parts of two formal business letters in this poem. Each letter informs the poet that she has failed—once in training for a job and once academically. What kind of job was she training for? What might her university major have been?

5. Certain words and phrases are repeated many times in the poem. Why do you think the poet did this?

6. There are a few phrases that are commonly found in this type of formal letter. Can you find them?

"Thinking Twice in the Laundromat"

7. Where is the poet when he notices the beautiful woman? Do you think he speaks to her?

8. Where does he imagine that she is from? What makes you think this?

9. Why does the poet imagine that she is married? (Find one piece of evidence in the poem.)

10. The poet has two fantasies about the woman and himself—one in *Bird Dance* and one in *Pink Blues*. What are these fantasies?

E. Freewriting.   Choose *one* of these topics. Write about it for fifteen minutes. Don't worry about grammar and don't use a dictionary. Just put as many ideas as you can on paper.

• your reaction to one of the poems

• a person or people from a part of the world that seems very **exotic** (strange, mysterious, and wonderful) to you

• a time you were once disappointed

• a time you were fascinated by a stranger

• a fantasy that you have had and the difference between it and reality

. . : : ⋮ ⋮ ⋮ **Part Two** Everyday English: Surviving Poetry

Before Listening

Thinking Ahead. **Group**   In the conversation in Part Two, a student is having difficulty in his American literature class. Before listening, discuss the answers to these questions.

1. In your culture, what do students do if they're having trouble in a class? List the possibilities.

2. Do you prefer **prose** (fiction and nonfiction) or poetry? Why? Is it possible for a poem to tell a story?

3. If you have studied poetry, did you analyze poems or write original poems?

4. Do you ever write poetry? If so, what are some themes of your poems?

 academic Strategy

Understanding Common Abbreviations

Each U.S. college class has a name (such as "English") and a course number. The course number usually indicates the level of the class, but the numbers vary slightly from one university to another.

Examples:

Course Numbers	Level
1–199	freshman (1st year)
200–299	sophomore (2nd year)
300–399	junior (3rd year)
400–499	senior (4th year)
500–599	graduate (5th–6th years)

In conversation, students often use these numbers or abbreviations for the names of their classes.

Examples: She's applying to <u>grad</u> school for next year.

I'm having trouble in my <u>lit</u> class. (=literature)

Have you taken <u>241</u> yet?

Practice. What do these common abbreviations probably mean?

anthro	chem	poli sci
biochem	econ	psych

Listening

A. Listening for the Main Idea. **Video/Audio**   In the scene that you're going to hear, Victor needs some help in his literature class. Listen to the entire conversation. As you listen, try to answer this question:

• What especially worries Victor about the poetry unit? (Find two things.)

B. Listening for Inferences. **Video/Audio**   Listen again to one segment of the conversation. Then answer these questions. Circle the letter of each answer.

1. Who is Pam?

    a. a friend of Victor's

    b. a professor in the English department

    c. Victor's American literature professor

    d. Dr. Sears' T. A. (teaching assistant)

2. If students are afraid that they might fail a class, what can they do?

    a. find a tutor to help them

    b. drop the class at any time

    c. drop the class before a certain **deadline** (the latest time to do something)

    d. drop the class before the final exam

3. What can you infer about Robert Frost and Maya Angelou?

   a. They are modern poets who write conversational poems.

   b. They are traditional poets who write poems with rhyme and rhythm.

   c. They write short stories and other prose.

   d. They are professors of literature.

C. Vocabulary: Guessing Meaning from Context. (Video/Audio) Listen again to one short
segment of the conversation. Then complete the sentences about the underlined words.

1. Two examples of <u>conventions</u> in poetry are _____

   and _____.

2. Writing that is <u>concise</u> has _____

   _____.

D. Listening for Important Details. (Video/Audio) Listen again to the segment from Exercise C.
Listen for some differences between older poetry and (most) contemporary poetry. Complete these
sentences.

1. Older or more traditional poetry has _____ and

   _____. Most contemporary poetry doesn't.

2. Much contemporary poetry is even _____, similar to

   _____, in some ways.

3. Contemporary poetry may seem difficult because it's more _____ than
   traditional poetry.

E. Listening to Poetry. Audio   Most poetry is more enjoyable when you *listen* to it. Here are two poems that you'll analyze and discuss. But right now, just listen and enjoy them. Read along silently if you want to.

A SUNDAY MORNING AFTER A SATURDAY NIGHT
by LoVerne Brown

She's so happy, this girl,
she's sending out sparks like a brush fire,
so lit with life
her eyes could beam airplanes through fog,
5 so warm with his loving
we could blacken our toast
on her forehead.

The phone rings
and she whispers to it
10 "I love you."
The cord uncoils
and leaps to tell him
she said it,
the receiver melts in her hand
15 as if done by Dali,
the whole room crackles

and we at the breakfast table
smile
but at a safe distance
20 having learned by living
that love so without insulation
can immolate more than the toast.

Without Stopping
by Cherry Jean Vasconcellos

In the dream
I can't stop crying.
Neighbors drop in.
They whisper while I
5 straighten pillows
on the couch,
my face wet
and silent as porcelain.
Later, my picture shows up
10 in supermarkets
nationwide: *Woman*
Never Quits Weeping.

In the real world,
he's gone two years
15 and I hardly ever cry.
Crude and shameless,
life has filled in the spaces
as it does with everyone.
Now, for example, I remember
20 how he touched me,
but I don't feel his hand
cup my hip the way I used to
in the first, bitter
euphoria after his death
25 when he rose up around me
like incense burning.

After Listening

A. Finding the Main Ideas.   Write your answers to these questions about the two poems on pages 76–77.

1. Which poem is about new love? _____

2. Which poem is about lost love? _____

3. Are these poems traditional or contemporary? (Use your answers to Exercise D on page 75 to

    help you with this.) _____

B. Vocabulary: Looking for Clues.   Without a dictionary, look back at the two poems to find words that mean the following.

"A Sunday Morning After a Saturday Night"

1. particles of fire thrown off by burning wood = _____

2. cooked bread = _____

3. becomes liquid = _____

4. makes many small, sudden, sharp noises = _____

5. something that protects one from heat = _____

6. destroy by fire = _____

"Without Stopping"

7. the thin, shiny material of fine quality cups and plates = _____

8. crying = _____

9. almost never = _____

10. curve one's hand in a rounded shape = _____

11. feeling of joy, great happiness = _____

12. something that smells sweet when it
     is burned (often for religious reasons) = _____

C. Looking for Clues: Meaning. `Group`   In the conversation, the
teaching assistant told Victor that a reader of poetry "needs to become
sort of a detective" to find clues to meaning. Now you will become
"detectives" and find clues to the meaning of these two poems. Study
the poems and answer these questions. When you finish, compare your
answers with those of other groups.

"A Sunday Morning After a Saturday Night"

1. The central image of this poem seems to be *heat*. Find at least
   three clues in the poem that support this.

   _____

   _____

   _____

2. What might be the age of the person in love? _____ Why do you think so?

   _____

3. Who are "we" (in line 17)? _____

4. What is "our" attitude toward "this girl"? _____

   _____

"Without Stopping"

5. Analyze the following lines from the poem to answer these questions.

   > Later, my picture shows up
   > in supermarkets
   > nationwide: *Woman*
   > *Never Quits Weeping.*

   a. Who is the woman? _____

   b. In her dream, there is a story about her in newspapers. How do you know this?

   _____

6. How do you know that this poem is about her lost lover or husband—not another person (such
   as a child, friend, or parent) whom she loves? _____

   _____

7. Why did she feel "euphoria" (line 24)? _____

_____

8. Why was the euphoria "bitter"? _____

_____

. : ⁝ ⁝ ⁝ **Part Three** The Mechanics of Listening
                                          and Speaking

Intonation

Statements and Questions `Audio`

Generally, the voice goes up at the end of *yes/no* questions (i.e., questions that can be answered by "yes" or "no") and down at the end of all other questions. Here are some examples:

Do you have a few minutes? ↗   How can I help? ↘

Could I make an appointment? ↗   What's giving you problems? ↘

Would it be possible on another day? ↗ When would you like to come in? ↘

In conversation, people often change a statement into a *yes/no* question simply by making their voice go up at the end. Here is an example:

Statement: You don't have anything earlier. ↘

Question: You don't have anything earlier? ↗

Even single-word statements can be changed into questions. The exact meaning depends on the context. Here are some examples:

Statements	Questions
Yes. = an answer	Yes? = "Really?" OR: "May I help you?"
Oh. = "I heard what you said."	Oh? = "Really?" OR: "Is that true?"

A. Practice. **Audio**   Listen to each sentence or word. Is it a statement or a question? Check (✓) the correct answer.

	Statement	Question			Statement	Question
1.	_____	_____	**5.**		_____	_____
2.	_____	_____	**6.**		_____	_____
3.	_____	_____	**7.**		_____	_____
4.	_____	_____	**8.**		_____	_____

Language Function

Questions with *Or* **Audio**

There are two types of questions with the word *or:* yes/no questions and *either/or* questions. The words are the same in both types of questions, but the intonation is different. *It's important to recognize the intonation because it determines what kind of answer is expected.* If the speaker's intonation goes up at the end of the sentence, then he or she is asking a *yes/no* question. If the speaker's intonation goes up and then down at the end of the sentence, he or she is asking an *either/or* question. Here are some examples:

A: Would you like to come in on Monday or Tuesday?
B: Yes.

A: Would you like to come in on Monday or Tuesday?
B: Monday.

B. Practice. **Audio**   Listen to each question. Circle the letter of the appropriate answer. Then wait a few seconds. You'll hear the answer on the tape.

1. *a.* Yes.

   b. Short stories.

2. *a.* No.

   b. Chapter Six.

3. *a.* No.

   b. Frost.

4. *a.* Yes, please.

   b. The term paper.

5. *a.* Yes.

   b. Saturday.

6. *a.* No, I'm not.

   b. World literature.

7. *a.* Sure.

   b. Thursday

8. *a.* No, not yet.

   b. the T. A.

C. Practice. **Audio**   Repeat the following questions and statements after the speaker.

1. *Yes/No* **Questions**

Do you have a few minutes?

Could I make an appointment?

Is that OK?

Will it be too late?

Would it be possible another day?

Wh- **Questions**

How can I help?

What's giving you problems?

When would you like to come in?

What do you think?

How did you do?

2. **Statements**

Yes.

Oh.

I can't.

It's not possible.

He doesn't like poetry.

Questions

Yes?

Oh?

I can't?

It's not possible?

He doesn't like poetry?

3. *Yes/No* **Questions**

Do you like poetry or novels?

Are you free Saturday or Sunday?

Did you talk with the professor or the T. A.?

Can you come in on Monday or Tuesday?

Have you studied American or British literature?

Either/Or **Questions**

Do you like poetry or novels?

Are you free Saturday or Sunday?

Did you talk with the professor or the T. A.?

Can you come in on Monday or Tuesday?

Have you studied American or British literature?

D. Practice. **Pair**   Work with a partner. Person A will ask the following questions, using *yes/no* intonation for some and *either/or* intonation for others. Person B will listen carefully and answer appropriately. Then exchange roles and do the exercise again.

1. Do you like poetry or novels?

2. Are you free Saturday or Sunday?

3. Did you talk with the professor or the T. A.?

4. Can you come in on Monday or Tuesday?

5. Have you studied American or British literature?

Language Function

Responding to a Negative Question: Agreeing (Audio)

In most languages, when people agree with a negative question, they say "yes" because they're thinking: "Yes. That's true." They are agreeing with the speaker. However, in English, the answer is "no." English speakers agree with the situation. Here is an example:

Q: You don't have anything earlier?

A: No.

After this "no," it's possible to add either a short answer or the correct information. Here is an example:

Q: You don't have anything earlier?

A: No, we don't.

OR:

A: No, I'm afraid we don't.

A: No, I'm sorry. We don't.

A: No. That's the only opening we have.

This is a difficult language function for most ESL/EFL students, but it's an important one to understand if you want to avoid the confusion and frustration of conversations like this:

Native English speaker:	You don't have one?
Nonnative English speaker:	Yes.
Native English speaker:	Oh, you *do* have one?
Nonnative English speaker:	No.
Native English speaker:	Oh, you mean you *don't* have one?
Nonnative English speaker:	Yes, I don't.*
Native English speaker:	Excuse me???

*Not possible grammar in English.

E. Practice. (Pair)   Person A will ask the following questions (with intonation rising at the end). Person B will agree and add a short answer.

1. It isn't possible?

2. You haven't studied Shakespeare?

3. He can't help us?

4. It wasn't hard?

5. You didn't understand it?

6. It wasn't too late to drop the class?

7. There isn't any class on Saturday?

8. She won't be here tomorrow?

F. Practice. (Pair)   Now exchange roles. (Person A becomes Person B.) Person A will ask these questions. Person B will agree and add a short answer.

1. You never studied poetry before?
2. We don't have to read Chapter Five?
3. This isn't difficult for you?
4. You don't like fiction?
5. They haven't ever been to Alaska?
6. She can't speak Urdu?
7. There isn't any opening on Tuesday?
8. They won't offer this class next term?

Language Function

Responding to a Negative Question: Disagreeing (Audio)

People ask negative questions (as in Exercises E and F) when they want confirmation; in other words, they *expect* the answer to be "no," but they're checking, just to make sure. However, sometimes they're incorrect, so the other person *dis*agrees. In such a case, the response is "yes." It's important to use emphasis in the voice. Notice the intonation in these sentences.

Q: You don't have any appointment earlier than 11:00?
A: *Yes, we do.*

Q: You haven't read it yet?
A: *Yes, I have.*

Q: We won't have to do a term paper?
A: *Yes, we will.*

It's also possible, after the "yes," to add the correct information. Here is an example:

Q: You don't have any appointment earlier than 11:00?
A: *Yes. Actually, we have an opening at 10:00.*

G. Practice. (Pair)   Go back and do Exercises E and F again. This time, Person B will *disagree* (say "yes") and add a short answer.

Pronunciation

The Medial *t* (Audio)

One challenge for ESL/EFL students is the medial *t*, or the *t* sound in the middle of many words. It's possible to pronounce it like this:

written   mountain   button

You'll sound more natural, however, if you pronounce it as most native speakers do:

written   mountain   button

H. Practice. **Audio**   Repeat these words after the speaker.

1. written   5. bitten

2. mountain   6. fountain

3. certain   7. forgotten

4. gotten   8. button

Language Function

Making Appointments/Negotiating Time **Audio**

When you make an appointment, it's often necessary to negotiate for a time different from the one first offered. Read along as you listen to this typical conversation.

A: Could I make an appointment for next week?

B: We have an opening at 3:00 on Tuesday.

A: Hmm. You don't have anything earlier?

B: No, I'm afraid not.

A: Um, well, I have classes Tuesday afternoon. Would it be possible in the morning or on another day?

B: Sure. How's 10:00 on Friday?

A: Great.

B: Okay. See you then.

A: Thanks a lot. Bye.

To make an appointment, there are several things you might say:

• Could I make an appointment for next week?

• I'd like to make an appointment, please.

• Is it possible to make an appointment with the doctor for next week?

There are several ways to negotiate time:

• I have classes in the afternoon. Is there any opening in the morning?

• That's a difficult time for me. Would it be possible at 10:00?

• Are there any appointments available in the morning?

• I'm afraid I can't make it at that time. Do you have something earlier?

Review: Language Functions

Making Appointments and Negotiating Time (Video/Audio)

Before you go on to the next activity, listen to these examples of making appointments. You'll use these functions in the next section.

Put It Together

Making Appointments and Negotiating Time

Role-Play. **Pair**   Use some of the structures in the box on page 85. With your partner, alternate roles. (In one conversation, Person A wants to make an appointment, and Person B is the receptionist. In the next conversation, Person A is the receptionist, and Person B needs to make an appointment.) Make appointments with these people:

- Your dentist
- Your department advisor at the university
- The financial aid officer at your school

⣿ Part Four Broadcast English: Interview with Poet Maya Angelou

Before Listening

A. Thinking Ahead. **Group**   You're going to listen to part of a radio interview with Maya Angelou, a poet and writer of prose. In the interview, she talks about an extraordinary incident that happened when she was a child of 7½, growing up in the black section of a town in the southern United States. Before you listen, discuss the answers to these questions.

1. Sometimes a child **stands out from the crowd**—is special or different in some way. What might be some reasons for this? Is it good or bad to stand out?

2. Some people have a terrible childhood due to poverty, serious illness, lack of love, loss of parents, or other reasons. However, most are able to survive, and some become healthy, happy, successful adults. What are some possible reasons for this? In other words, how are they able to rise above tragedy?

3. The interviewer says, "Words *do* have enormous power." Have you ever said something that made a big change in someone's life? Has someone ever said something that made a big change in your life? If so, was it a good change or a bad change?

B. Vocabulary Preparation.
The people in the interview use some words and expressions that may be new to you. First, read each sentence and guess the meaning of the underlined words. Then choose their meaning from the definitions in the box. Write the letters in the blanks.

Sentences

_____ **1.** She was very different from the others in the group, and they didn't include her in their activities, so she began to feel like a <u>pariah</u>.

_____ **2.** In many countries, people of minority racial or religious groups suffer from <u>discrimination</u> from the rest of society.

_____ **3.** His success can be <u>credited to</u> his education.

_____ **4.** The woman was <u>raped</u> by a man in the neighborhood. She was so traumatized by this that she refused to name the man. Finally, after pressure from her family, she told the police who the man was.

_____ **5.** He committed a crime. <u>Subsequently</u>, the police found him and arrested him.

_____ **6.** Years and years of reading is <u>apt</u> preparation for someone who wants to become a writer.

_____ **7.** He was a man of peace. However, when he saw hatred and injustice all around him, he had to stop himself—with difficulty—from committing violence. This was a terrible <u>crucible</u> for him.

_____ **8.** When I was a child, I used to put a blanket over the kitchen table and then <u>crawl</u> under the table. It was great—like a cave, my own secret place.

_____ **9.** With a bit of food, I <u>lured</u> the frightened cat from her hiding place.

Definitions
a. serious test or trial
b. sexually attacked
c. outsider; person thrown out of society
d. after that
e. actively attracted
f. believed to be the result of
g. move on hands and knees
h. prejudice; treatment against a person or group of people
i. appropriate

Listening

A. Listening for Main Ideas. `Audio`   As you listen to
the interview the first time, try to answer these questions:

Maya Angelou

- Why did Maya Angelou stop speaking?

- How did this indirectly lead to her becoming a poet?

 listening Strategy

Understanding the Passive Voice `Audio`

People often use the passive voice in these cases:

- They don't know who did an action.

- They know who did an action, but they don't want to say who it was.

- It isn't important for the listener to know who did an action.

Here are some examples:

Someone hurt her. (active voice) =
    She <u>was hurt</u>. (passive voice)

My brother committed a crime. (active voice) =
    A crime <u>was committed</u>. (passive voice)

Several people encouraged her to read. (active voice) =
    She <u>was encouraged</u> to read. (passive voice)

Less commonly used but still important to understand is the use of passive gerunds. Like gerunds, which are used as nouns, passive gerunds are used as noun phrases. Here are some examples:

<u>Being introduced</u> to poetry changed her entire life.
    (= She was introduced to poetry, and this changed her entire life.)

His parents were upset about <u>his being expelled</u> from school.
    (= He was expelled from school, and his parents were upset about this.)

B. Practice. (Audio)   Listen again to what is probably the central part of Angelou's story. As you listen, fill in the blanks with the passive voice.

Well, um, I—at 7½ I _____, and, uh, I said so. I mean, I after pressure
                                            1
from my brother, who I loved a lot, I named the man. Um, the man _____
                                                                                                  2
subsequently _____, I mean, almost immediately. And, uh, I believed that
                                  2
because I had spoken, ah, the man was dead. And it _____ that he
                                                                                       3
_____ to death. Uh, I thought that my saying his name caused directly his
                      4
_____, and I guess it is so.
              5

C. Listening for Inferences. (Audio)   Listen again to two short segments. Then write your answers to these questions.

1. What can you infer about society in Angelou's "little town"?

    _____

2. In your opinion, why is Angelou careful to use the passive voice five times in this short passage?

    _____

D. Listening for Details. (Audio)   Read over these questions. Write brief answers to some of them now. Then listen again to the interview and answer the rest of the questions.

1. What two things "almost directly" helped Angelou to survive a difficult childhood? _____

    _____

2. What is a "volunteer mute"? _____

3. Why did Angelou become a volunteer mute? _____

    _____

4. Why wasn't she afraid to speak to her brother? _____

    _____

5. Why did Mrs. Flowers say Angelou "must speak" poetry—read it aloud? _____

    _____

6. How did Angelou begin to speak again? _____

    _____

listening Strategy

Hearing Rhyme and Rhythm (Audio)

In the conversation in Part Two, the student mentioned *rhyme* and *rhythm*. These are two conventions in some poetry. Rhyme refers to the sound of two or more words when stressed vowels (*a, e, i, o, u*) and the consonants after them are the same. Here are some examples:

cost/lost   pain/stain

Rhythm is the order of stressed and unstressed syllables. In some poems it is regular and predictable; in others it is not. The rhythm of a poem can be shown with stress marks (ˊ) over stressed syllables and rounded marks (˘) over unstressed syllables. Here is an example:

The breezes taste

Of apple peel.

The air is full

Of smells to feel   —John Updike, "September"

Source: John Updike, excerpt from "September" from *A Child's Calendar.* Copyright © 1965 by John Updike and Nancy Burkert. Reprinted with the permission of Holiday House, Inc.

E. Listening to Poetry. (Audio)   Here is a poem by Maya Angelou that you'll analyze and discuss. Right now just listen to the "music" of the poem. Read along if you want to. Don't worry about new words.

Caged Bird

by Maya Angelou

A free bird leaps
on the back of the wind
and floats downstream
till the current ends
5 and dips his wing
in the orange sun rays
and dares to claim the sky.

But a bird that stalks
down his narrow cage
10 can seldom see through
his bars of rage
his wings are clipped and
his feet are tied
so he opens his throat to sing.

15 The caged bird sings
with a fearful trill
of things unknown
but longed for still
and his tune is heard
20 on the distant hill
for the caged bird
sings of freedom.

The free bird thinks of another breeze
and the trade winds soft through the sighing trees
25 and the fat worms waiting on a dawn-bright lawn
and he names the sky his own.

But a caged bird stands on the grave of dreams
his shadow shouts on a nightmare scream
his wings are clipped and his feet are tied
30 so he opens his throat to sing.

The caged bird sings
with a fearful trill
of things unknown
but longed for still
35 and his tune is heard
on the distant hill
for the caged bird
sings of freedom.

After Listening

A. Discussion: Finding Connections. Pair   You know that Maya Angelou became a poet. In
a strange and terrible way, it appears that her rape as a child was, indirectly, the first step toward "finding
her voice" as a poet. What were the other steps? Fill them in on this map.

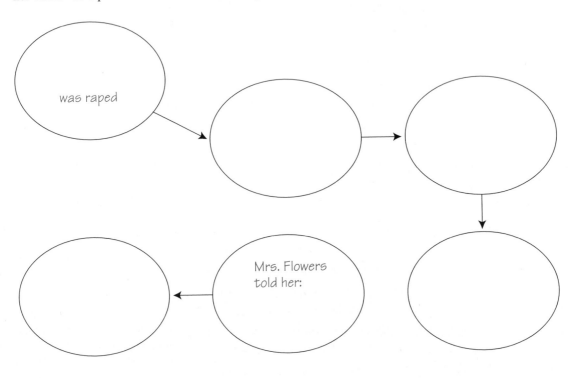

B. Discussion: "Caged Bird." Group   Analyze the poem "Caged Bird" by answering the follow-
ing questions. When you finish, compare your answers with those of other groups.

1. Say aloud the word at the end of each line. Does it rhyme with another word at the end of a
   different line in that **stanza** (group of lines)? Write here the words that rhyme.

   cage = rage   _____   _____

2. Find the rhythm in the last stanza. Mark the stressed (´) and unstressed (˘) syllables.

3. Do you think that the style of "Caged Bird" is traditional or modern? Why do you think this?

4. In the poem, which kind of bird sings? Why?

5. What might the two different birds be symbolic of?

. : : : : : **Part Five** Academic English: American Poets

Before Listening

A. Thinking Ahead. **Group**   You're going to listen to a lecture about American poets. Before listening, discuss the answers to these questions.

1. Have you studied or read poetry in your own language? If so, is there any characteristic that most poets in that language share? In other words, do they have anything in common?

2. It often takes many years for a poet to find his or her voice—a specific, unique style of expression. Can you think of poets in your native language who have a unique voice? If so, can you describe this voice?

3. The lecturer explains three of the **creative impulses** in American poetry—three reasons that people write poetry, three types of inspiration. In your opinion, why do people write poetry? For a few minutes, brainstorm possible impulses that lead people to create poetry. Write them in the blanks.

_____   _____

_____   _____

_____   _____

_____   _____

B. Guessing Meaning from Context.   In the lecture, you are going to hear some words that may be new to you. Before you listen, guess the meanings of some words from the lecture. The words are underlined in the sentences. Look for clues to their meanings in the words around them.

Write your guess in the blank after each sentence. Then check your guess with your teacher or the dictionary.

1. I can't give you an example of a "typical" American poet because these poets are a very <u>diverse</u> group.

   Guess: _____

2. Although he now writes mostly prose—both fiction and nonfiction—he began by writing <u>verse</u>.

   Guess: _____

3. Nobody knew much about him because he had withdrawn from society and become a <u>recluse</u>. He led a solitary life for many years.

   Guess: _____

4. William Saroyan's short stories have an <u>idiosyncratic</u> use of punctuation. For example, he never uses quotation marks at all. This is highly unusual, and Saroyan is the only writer I know who does this.

   Guess: _____

5. Even if you don't understand the language, you can identify his poems at a <u>glance</u> because of the way they look on the page.

   Guess: _____

6. Since the <u>advent</u> of the computer and the Internet, people have had far greater access to information that was difficult to find before.

   Guess: _____

7. She had very strong <u>convictions</u> about the importance of freedom and <u>egalitarianism</u>. It was her belief that people couldn't really be free if they didn't also have equality with everyone else in society.

   Guess: (convictions) _____

   Guess: (egalitarianism) _____

8. In his poetry he <u>incorporated</u> the rhythms of jazz, religious gospel music, and the blues.

   Guess: _____

9. She <u>disguised</u> her own identity in order to feel free to express her feelings. Nobody realized she was really writing about herself.

   Guess: _____

10. For many years, he went through <u>psychoanalysis</u>. His therapist helped him to <u>grapple</u> with his personal psychological demons, but it was a long, hard struggle.

    Guess: (psychoanalysis) _____

    Guess: (grapple) _____

C. Using Abbreviations.   The following is a list of words that you'll hear often in the lecture. Decide on your own abbreviation for each.

Words in the Lecture   **My Abbreviations**

1. American   _____

2. poet   _____

3. poetry   _____

4. impulse   _____

5. conviction   _____

6. rhythm   _____

7. voice   _____

Listening

A. Recognizing Names.   **Audio**   Listen to the speaker pronounce these names of poets mentioned in the lecture. Notice the spelling so that you'll be able to take notes more easily.

   John Berryman   Emily Dickinson   Anne Sexton

    e.e. cummings   Langston Hughes   Walt Whitman

B. Vocabulary: Words in Literature.   **Audio**   Listen to one short segment of the lecture "American Poets." What does the lecturer mean by the term *wordplay*?

Wordplay means _____

_____

 academic Strategy

Getting the Main Ideas in a Lecture   **Audio**

A well-organized speaker often makes the main idea clear by repeating it, in somewhat different words, several times during a lecture: in the introduction, at the end of each major section, and again in the conclusion.

Practice.   In the lecture that follows, pay special attention to the repetition of three main ideas.

C. Listening for the Main Idea. **Audio**   Listen once to the entire lecture. (You'll listen again later.) Follow along with the outline. Then write the answer to this question.

- What are three impulses that create voice in American poetry?

American Poets

I. Introduction: Three Impulses That Create Voice in American Poetry

   A. Pleasure of wordplay _____

   B. _____

   C. _____

II. Creative Impulse: _____

   A. Poet: _____

        1. Background info. abt. her:

            a. Woman, 19th century, recluse

            b. _____

        2. Use of punctuation

            a. _____

            b. _____

   B. Poet: _____

        1. Background info. abt. him:

            a. _____

            b. _____

        2. Use of punctuation (possible because of the typewriter)

            a. _____

            b. Squeezed, stretched, separated words, phrases, and lines

III. Creative Impulse: _____

   A. Poet: _____

        1. Background info. abt. him:

            a. _____

            b. _____

            c. _____

    2. Wanted his poems to express _____

_____

    3. Masterpiece: "Song of Myself"

        a. _____

        b. _____

        c. _____

B. Poet: _____

    1. Background info. abt. him:

        a. Mem. of the Harlem Renaissance (a literary movement), which celebrated

           _____

           _____

           _____

        b. _____

    2. Used the voices of peo. he knew & portrayed _____

_____

IV. Creative Impulse: _____

A. Poet: _____

    1. Background info. abt. him:

        a. _____

        b. _____

    2. His poetry

        a. In the voice of "Henry"

        b. Book *Dream Song*—an attempt to help him w/ _____

           _____

B. Poet: _____

    1. Reason for writing poetry: _____

_____

    2. Her poetry _____

_____

V. Conclusion

A. Primary creative impulse

B. But _____

_____

D. Listening for Important Details. (Audio) Listen to the entire lecture again. This time, fill in the rest of the outline with the names of poets who exemplify (are good examples of) each creative impulse and with information about each poet.

E. (Optional) Filling in the Gaps. (Audio) Listen one last time to the entire lecture and fill in any gaps in your outline.

F. Extension. (Audio) In the lecture, you were introduced to six well-known U.S. poets. Listen to these poems (and one excerpt from a very long poem) written by these six people. Read along silently as you listen to the "music" in each poem. Don't worry about the words that you don't understand.

"Hope" is the thing with feathers—

That perches in the soul—

And sings the tune without the words—

And never stops—at all—

5 And sweetest—in the Gale—is heard—

And sore must be the storm—

That could abash the little Bird

That kept so many warm—

I've heard it in the chillest land—

10 And on the strangest Sea—

Yet, never, in Extremity,

It asked a crumb—of Me.

—Emily Dickinson

Source: Emily Dickinson, 254 ["'Hope' is the thing with feathers"] from *The Poems of Emily Dickinson,* edited by Thomas H. Johnson. Copyright © 1951, 1955, 1979, 1983 by The President and Fellows of Harvard College. Reprinted with the permission of The Belknap Press of Harvard University Press.

Portrait

by e. e. cummings

Buffalo Bill's
defunct
    who used to
    ride a watersmooth-silver
5   stallion
and break onetwothreefourfive pigeonsjustlikethat
                                Jesus
he was a handsome man
                  and what i want to know is
10 how do you like your blueeyed boy
Mister Death

Song of Myself (excerpt)

by Walt Whitman

The smoke of my own breath,
Echoes, ripples, buzz'd whispers, love-root, silk-thread, crotch and vine,
My respiration and inspiration, the beating of my heart, the passing of blood and
    air through my lungs,
5 The sniff of green leaves and dry leaves, and of the shore and dark-color'd sea-rocks,
    and of hay in the barn,
The sound of the belch'd words of my voice loos'd to the eddies of the wind,
A few light kisses, a few embraces, a reaching around of arms,
The play of shine and shade on the trees as the supple boughs wag,
10 The delight alone or in the rush of the streets, or along the fields and hill-sides,
The feeling of health, the full-moon trill, the song of me rising from bed and
    meeting the sun.
Have you reckon'd a thousand acres much? have you reckon'd the earth much?
Have you practic'd so long to learn to read?
15 Have you felt so proud to get at the meaning of poems?

Jazz Band in a Parisian Cabaret

by Langston Hughes

Play that thing,
Jazz band!
Play it for the lords and ladies,
For the dukes and counts,
5   For the whores and gigolos,
For the American millionaires,
And the schoolteachers
Out for a spree.
Play it,
10 Jazz band!
You know that tune
That laughs and cries at the same time.
You know it.
     May I?
15   Mais oui.
     Mein Gott!
     Parece una rumba.
Play it, jazz band!
You've got seven languages to speak in
20 And then some,
Even if you do come from Georgia.
     Can I go home wid yuh, sweetie?
     Sure.

Source: Langston Hughes, "Jazz Band in a Parisian Cabaret" from *The Collected Poems of Langston Hughes,* edited by Arnold Rampersad and David Roessel. Copyright © 1994 by the Estate of Langston Hughes. Reprinted with the permission of Alfred A. Knopf, Inc. and Harold Ober Associates.

He Resigns

by John Berryman

Age, and the deaths, and the ghosts.
Her having gone away
in spirit from me. Hosts
of regrets come & find me empty.

5 I don't feel this will change.
I don't want any thing
or person, familiar or strange.
I don't think I will sing

10 any more just now;
or ever. I must start
to sit with a blind brow
above an empty heart.

Words

by Anne Sexton

Be careful of words,
even the miraculous ones.
For the miraculous we do our best,
sometimes they swarm like insects
5 and leave not a sting but a kiss.
They can be as good as fingers.
They can be as trusty as the rock
you stick your bottom on.
But they can be both daisies and bruises.

10 Yet I am in love with words.
They are doves falling out of the ceiling.
They are six holy oranges sitting in my lap.
They are the trees, the legs of summer,
and the sun, its passionate face.

15 Yet often they fail me.
I have so much I want to say,
so many stories, images, proverbs, etc.
But the words aren't good enough,
the wrong ones kiss me.
20 Sometimes I fly like an eagle
but with the wings of a wren.

But I try to take care
and be gentle to them.
Words and eggs must be handled with care.
25 Once broken they are impossible
things to repair.

After Listening

A. Using Your Notes.   Answer these questions from your notes. When you finish, compare your answers with a partner's.

1. Which two poets wrote for highly personal and psychological reasons?

    _____

2. Which two poets are known for their unique and challenging use of punctuation?

    _____

3. Which two poets represented the diversity of American society?

    _____

B. Discussion. **Group**   Discuss the answers to these questions about the poems on pages 98–101.

1. Is there one poem that you especially like? If so, what do you like about it?

2. Try to find an example in each poem of the characteristics that you heard about in the lecture.

C. Applying Your Knowledge.   Look back at the three poems in Part One, pages 68–71. Which two poems make use of wordplay? Which two represent ethnic diversity in the society? How are all three also personal expressions?

 Step Beyond

 speaking Strategy

Giving a Speech to the Class

You will occasionally need to give a speech in front of the class. These suggestions will help you give an effective presentation.

*   Prepare, prepare, prepare. Organize your ideas and write your speech as you would organize an essay.

*   Don't memorize what you are going to say. If necessary, though, you might memorize short pieces. For example, you might memorize a quotation or a few lines of a poem.

- Put *just notes* on 3 × 5 index cards. These notes might be the first few words of each section of your speech, or they might be phrases that you are afraid you will forget.
- Practice your speech several times at home. Present your speech to a friend or family member or even to your bathroom mirror.
- During your speech, glance at your index cards whenever you need help remembering something.
- As you're speaking, have eye contact with the people in your audience, the people to whom you're speaking. If it makes you nervous to have eye contact, look at people's foreheads instead of their eyes.
- Don't forget to breathe.

A. Choosing a Topic.   You're going to give a speech or presentation to the class. Choose *one* of the following projects.

Project 1: Write your own poem.

Project 2: Tell about a person or event that changed your life.

Project 3: Analyze one poem written in English.

B. Preparing and Giving Your Presentation.   Follow these steps for your project.

Project 1: Write your own poem.

To help you do this, you might follow some of the suggestions from the conversation in Part Two: 1) begin by relating a dream that you've had; 2) describe an old family photo as if you were one of the people in it (not yourself); or 3) try writing with your left hand (if you're right-handed) or with your right hand (if you're left-handed). You might also write a poem about an event in the news, something that has happened in your life, or a reaction to something that you've learned in class.
    Choose *one* of these creative impulses for your poem:

- wordplay
- an important characteristic of your society
- personal or private experience

    Read your poem to the class or memorize it and recite it. Afterwards, briefly (1–2 minutes) tell the class about the experience of writing this poem: How did you get the idea for it? What gave you problems? What did you learn from the experience?

Project 2: Tell about a person or event that changed your life.

To help you begin, think of the radio passage in Part Four. Maya Angelou related the story of one person, Mrs. Flowers, who changed Angelou's life by encouraging her to read poetry aloud.

Now think back over your life. Think about the people who have influenced you and the events that have shaped your life. Choose one person *or* one event. Here are just some suggestions:

People

- a family member
- a friend
- a teacher
- a person in the news
- a person you've read about

Events

- something tragic
- something funny
- a small incident that gave you a big idea
- an event in the recent history of your country

Give a short speech (2–3 minutes) about this person or event. Follow the guidelines in the box on pages 102–103 to prepare and give your speech.

Project 3: Analyze a poem.

Choose one poem, written in English, that you like and have some ideas about. Alternatively, you can choose two poems to compare. To find your poem(s), go to the library. Your teacher might suggest several poets, or you might choose one or two of the poets from this chapter. Look through books of poetry to find something that you especially like. Make a copy of the poem(s) for each class member.

Prepare and give a short speech (2–3 minutes) about your poem(s). Follow the guidelines in the box on pages 102–103. Before speaking about the poem, have the class read the poem silently as you read it aloud. In preparing your analysis, include:

- the poet's background (if possible)
- the creative impulse for writing the poem
- your ideas about the images or symbols in the poem
- your ideas about the meaning of the poem

 *listening* Strategy

Listening to a Speech or Presentation

Be an active listener when a class member is giving a presentation! Remember how difficult it is for most people to stand in front of the class. Try to make it as comfortable as possible for the speaker. You can do this by *paying attention* and occasionally nodding or smiling at an appropriate moment. Have a pencil and a piece of paper on your desk. Jot down (write quickly) any question that comes to mind during the speech or anything that you especially like about the presentation. Save your questions and comments for after the presentation.

C. Responding to a Presentation. Take brief notes during each student's presentation. Be prepared, in case there is time to do so, either to ask a question or tell the speaker what you enjoyed about the presentation.

chapter Four

Heroes and Survivors

In this chapter, you'll read several American folktales. You'll listen to a conversation about film heroes, a radio interview about a new anthology of African American literature, and a lecture about heroes in American folk stories. You'll also discuss heroes from the folklore of your culture.

Part One Introduction: American Tall Tales

A. Thinking Ahead. (Pair)   You're going to read two "tall tales"—traditional folk stories that are "bigger than life." In most cultures, we first encounter such folk stories when we are children and absorb with them, subconsciously, information about our culture. The author of most folk stories is anonymous; nobody knows who first told them. These two stories were written early in the twentieth century, but as with most folklore, there are different versions of the same story. The stories here combine many versions.

Before you read, try to answer these questions.

1. In your culture, do people enjoy telling folk stories? If so, in what situations? (At home? Around a campfire?) Can anyone tell these stories, or are they told only by certain famous storytellers? How old are your most famous folk stories? Do children read folk stories in school?

2. Many American folk stories involve the theme of the westward movement into the **wilderness**— the vast empty spaces of the frontier—and of the attempt to **tame the frontier**—in other words, to bring civilization to the wilderness. What is a common theme in the folklore of your culture?

B. Reading.   As you read these tall tales, consider how they reflected American culture of the past.

Paul Bunyan

One day, long ago, when this country was still young, a remarkable baby was born in the northeastern state of Maine. He was a giant of a baby. At two weeks of age, Paul Bunyan weighed 200 pounds. He grew so fast that his parents had to move his bed outside. They realized that soon he wouldn't
5 fit through the door. After one more week, Paul couldn't fit in his bed. The neighbors got together and built a ship, which they floated in the ocean just off the shore. This ship became Paul's bed, and every few hours his parents would row out to him with boatloads of food.

This system worked well for a while. Then Paul began to get restless, and
10 when he moved around in his ship, he created such huge waves that three towns along the coast were washed away. After that, his family had to take Paul and move west.

Paul Bunyan grew up to become the first and most famous lumberjack in the land—and also the largest. He was so large that he combed his beard with
15 a pine tree.

Together with his giant blue ox, Babe, he began the timber industry. He hired a team of lumberjacks, and they cut down so many trees to provide tim-
20 ber for towns in the growing country that every week they had to move the entire camp to a town farther west. Paul put wheels on the camp buildings so that Babe the Blue Ox could pull the
25 whole camp from state to state, deeper into the wilderness.

Paul Bunyan certainly left his mark on the land. For example, the lumberjacks who worked for him liked maple syrup on their breakfast pancakes; in order to move boatloads of maple syrup from Vermont to his lumber camps in
30 the west, he had to dig the St. Lawrence River. If a road was too crooked, Paul simply hitched Babe to the road and had her pull. That straightened out the road right away. And once, after cutting down a forest in the west, Paul Bunyan was a little tired. As he dragged his axe along the ground behind him, the axe made a mark in the ground. You can still see this mark today, in Arizona. We
35 call it the Grand Canyon.

Pecos Bill

Any creature living near the Pecos River can tell you that the best cowboy who ever lived was Pecos Bill.

When Bill was a little baby, he was already as tough as nails. His family was living on their ranch in east Texas when another family moved in fifty miles away. Well, Bill's
5 pa decided that the neighborhood was getting just *too* crowded, so the whole family packed up and started moving west.

One day, while the family was crossing the wide desert of west Texas, little Bill fell out of the
10 back of the wagon. Nobody noticed he wasn't there until it was too late. Bill was sitting there in the dirt when a coyote came along. This creature decided that Bill must be a lost little coyote, so she picked him up by the scruff of his neck and took
15 him back to her den.

So it was that Pecos Bill grew up among coyotes. He learned the ways of nature, and he learned to talk with the creatures. It was a fine life. Then one day, seventeen years later, a cowboy was riding through the desert when he saw Pecos Bill. It's hard to say who was more surprised.

20   "Who are you?" the cowboy asked.

"Coyote," said Bill.

"No you ain't," said the cowboy. "You're a cowboy, just like me."

Pecos Bill considered this. He had sometimes suspected that he was a little different from the other coyotes. Maybe this was the reason.

25   Sadly, he said goodbye to his coyote family and friends and rode off to be with the cowboys. He had to learn how to wear clothes, take an occasional bath, and be a regular cowboy. Bill learned most things very quickly. It was certainly easier than learning to be a coyote—except for the baths.

One night he heard some of the cowboys talking about a dangerous gang of
30 outlaws, the Hell's Gate Gang, which was creating all sorts of trouble in west Texas. Pecos Bill decided to do something about this. He jumped on his horse and set out to find them. He figured he could tame these outlaws the same way he tamed a wild horse.

On his way to find the outlaws, he ran into a few obstacles. First, there was no
35 water at all on his long journey because he was traveling across the desert during a terrible drought; there had been no rain for years, and Texas was drying up and blowing away. Soon Texas would be as small as Rhode Island.

Then, along the way, his horse broke her ankle, so Bill had to sling the poor creature around his shoulders and carry her. After walking a few hundred miles, he ran
40 into a deadly rattlesnake. It was at least fifty feet long, and it wanted to have Bill for dinner. It wrapped itself around Bill and squeezed and squeezed. But Bill just squeezed back even harder until all the poison was squeezed right out of that rattler. Then he made a neat coil of the rattlesnake and put it over his arm. So it was that Pecos Bill invented
45 the first *lariat*—the rope that became as important to all cowboys as their horse or gun.

After a few hundred more miles of walking, Pecos Bill neared the camp of the Hell's Gate Gang. Now, the outlaws didn't even no-
50 tice him at first because they were staring at something else that was coming their way— *fast*—the biggest, meanest tornado that had ever hit Texas. Well, Pecos Bill looked up into the sky and saw this terrible black funnel cloud.

55 He took the rattlesnake, made a careful loop with it, and began to swing it in huge circles over his head. Yelling the loudest war whoop that anyone had ever heard, he swung that lariat and grabbed the tornado. The tornado pulled him up into the sky, but he held on and rode it just like a wild horse. He rode and rode and pulled the lariat tighter and tighter until all the rain was squeezed

60 out. That day it rained over Texas, Oklahoma, New Mexico, and Arizona. Finally, the tornado was all tired out. Pecos Bill slipped off the tornado over California. He fell so hard that the ground level sank and created Death Valley,

65 which, as everyone knows, is 200 feet below sea level.

The outlaws were astonished. They decided right then that Pecos Bill would be their boss and that they would give up the outlaw life. They

70 learned from him how to swing a rope to capture wild longhorn cattle, and that was the beginning of cattle ranches.

But Pecos Bill's coyote family missed him terribly. To this day, whenever you hear a coyote howling at the moon, you know that it's calling sadly for Bill to return.

C. Vocabulary Check.   Find words in the stories that mean the following:

Paul Bunyan

1. a person who works in a forest and cuts down trees = _____

2. wood for building = _____

3. not straight = _____

4. a tool for cutting trees = _____

Pecos Bill

5. criminals = _____

6. to make gentle or civilized = _____

7. difficulties; something that prevents success = _____

8. long time with no rain = _____

9. a dangerous, violent wind that spins around = _____

10. making a long, loud cry = _____

D. Analyzing the Reading.   Many tall tales are an attempt to explain the existence of natural phenomena or cultural features. What explanations can you find in these two American tall tales? Write them on the chart.

	Natural Phenomena or Cultural Features	**Why These Exist or How They Began**
Paul Bunyan		
Pecos Bill		

E. Discussion.   Group   Discuss the answers to these questions.

1. In what ways do the stories of Paul Bunyan and Pecos Bill reflect American culture or history?

2. In your culture, are there any folk stories that explain the existence of geological formations such as rivers, deserts, or mountains? Do any folk stories explain how some cultural feature began? If so, tell your group about them.

F. Freewriting.   Choose *one* of these topics. Write about it for fifteen minutes. Don't worry about grammar and don't use a dictionary. Just put as many ideas as you can on paper.

• your reaction to the folk story "Paul Bunyan" or "Pecos Bill"

• your favorite hero from the folklore of your culture

• an explanation from folklore of a geological formation in your country

. : : : : **Part Two** Everyday English: Movie Heroes

Before Listening

A. Brainstorming. **Class**   Take a few minutes and brainstorm names of **westerns** (movies about the so-called American Wild West) and film stars from these westerns. On the board, write as many as you can think of. Then brainstorm names of recent **blockbuster** movies—expensively produced and widely popular films—and their stars. Write them on the board.

B. Thinking Ahead. **Group**   In most movies, there is a **protagonist**—a central character who is usually a hero or heroine. In some movies, this character is an **antihero**—not a "bad guy" necessarily, but rather a protagonist who lacks some of the moral qualities of a typical hero. Discuss what you know about protagonists.

1. Which actors* usually play a hero? What characteristics do you associate with a hero (female or male)? List them.

2. Which actors have played antiheroes over the last twenty years? What characteristics do you associate with antiheroes? List them.

    *Note: The word *actor* can refer to either a male or female.

*The Seven
Samurai*

*The Magnificent
Seven*

C. Vocabulary Preparation.

You are going to hear the students use some expressions that are common in the context of film. First, read each sentence and guess the meaning of the underlined words. Then choose their meaning from the definitions in the box. Write the letters in the blanks.

Sentences

_____ **1.** In *The Magnificent Seven,* the character played by Yul Brynner has six <u>allies</u> with him when he rides into town.

_____ **2.** The ending to the movie is <u>ambiguous</u>, so we argued for a long time about what it meant.

_____ **3.** The Japanese film *The Seven Samurai* <u>paved the way for</u> the American film *The Magnificent Seven,* which was filmed several years later.

_____ **4.** In many westerns, there's an <u>eye-for-an-eye sort of justice</u>.

_____ **5.** When the stranger first came to town, we were all very curious about him. He didn't talk much and seemed to be a <u>loner</u>.

_____ **6.** My favorites are the <u>spaghetti westerns</u> with background music by Ennio Morricone.

_____ **7.** For a few years the family moved, <u>rootless</u>, from country to country.

> **Definitions**
>
> *a.* made possible
>
> *b.* people who help or support
>
> *c.* person who chooses to spend a lot of time alone
>
> *d.* movies about the American Wild West that are actually filmed in Italy
>
> *e.* punishment for criminals that causes them to suffer as their victims suffered
>
> *f.* without a home
>
> *g.* unclear; understood in more than one way

Listening

A. Listening for the Main Idea. (Video/Audio)   You're going to hear three students talk about movies. Listen to the entire conversation. As you listen, try to answer this question:

• What kind of movies does Victor like?

B. Listening for Details. (Video/Audio)   Listen again to the conversation. Then write your answers to these questions. Write short phrases, not complete sentences.

1. What kind of character does Clint Eastwood play in *A Fistful of Dollars?* _____

_____

2. What film is *A Fistful of Dollars* based on? _____

_____

3. How did the kind of character in spaghetti westerns influence recent movies? _____

_____

_____

4. What does Chrissy think about these recent movies? _____

_____

5. What does Brandon think about them? _____

_____

After Listening

A. Taking a Survey. (Class)   Move around the classroom and interview other students. (In addition, for homework your teacher might have you interview other people in your school or neighborhood.) Find out what people think about movie heroes. Ask the following questions and record the answers on the chart on page 114.

• Consider one of your favorite movies. Describe the protagonist. (What qualities does this character possess?) Is the protagonist a hero or antihero?

• Is this movie from your country? If not, what country is it from?

• Does the protagonist represent qualities that are valued in your culture?

	Person 1 Country: _____	Person 2 Country: _____	Person 3 Country: _____	Person 4 Country: _____	Person 5 Country: _____
Favorite movie					
Qualities of the protagonist					
Country					
Represents values in your culture?					

B. Discussing Survey Results. Group   Discuss what you learned from your survey. First, share your charts with your group. Then answer these questions.

1. Are certain movies especially popular? If so, what are they?

2. Are most of the protagonists truly heroes, or are they antiheroes?

3. Do people seem attracted to protagonists who represent the ideals of their own culture or who represent the ideals of a different culture?

⠄⠆⠒⠒⠒ **Part Three** The Mechanics of Listening and Speaking

Language Function

Starting a Conversation `Audio`

There are several ways to start a conversation with someone you know. One way is to ask a question about what the person has been doing lately. Here are some examples:

- What have you been doing lately?
- What have you guys been up to lately?
- So what's new?
- How was your weekend?

Friends give each other honest answers; the answer usually leads to more conversation. Here is an example:

A: What have you been doing lately?

B: I was at the library all weekend. I have a big exam next week.

  OR:

  Well, I saw a great movie last night.

  Um, I went to the beach on Sunday.

Either Speaker A or Speaker B can continue the conversation by asking another question. Here are some examples:

A: What have you been doing lately?

B: Well, I saw a great movie last night.

A: Oh . . . what did you see?

A: How was your weekend?

B: Great. How was yours?

Intonation

Review: Question Intonation Audio

In Chapter Three, you saw that your voice goes up at the end of *yes/no* questions, and down at the end of *wh-* questions. Here are some examples:

Did you do anything interesting this weekend?

What did you do this weekend?

When you hear a *yes/no* question, the speaker expects an answer beginning with *yes* or *no*. When you hear a *wh-* question, the speaker expects a longer, more informative answer.

In casual conversation, a *yes/no* question doesn't always begin with *Do/Does* or *Did:* In using this structure, the speaker is asking for confirmation of what he/she already thinks is true. Here is an example:

You went to the beach this weekend?

A. Practice. Audio   Listen to the difference between *yes/no* and *wh-* questions. For each question you hear, indicate whether the speaker expects a *yes* or *no* answer or an information answer. Circle your choice.

1.	Yes	No	Information	**4.**	Yes	No	Information
2.	Yes	No	Information	**5.**	Yes	No	Information
3.	Yes	No	Information	**6.**	Yes	No	Information

B. Practice. Pair   Now practice *yes/no* and *wh-* question intonation. Ask your partner each question. Pay attention to correct intonation. Your partner will answer. Then exchange roles.

1. What did you do this weekend?

2. How was your weekend?

3. Did you see a movie last night?

4. You saw a Clint Eastwood movie?

5. What have you been doing lately?

6. You're going to the library tonight?

Pronunciation

Reduced Forms of *Wh-* questions Audio

When people speak naturally, some words (and combinations of sounds) become reduced, or short-ened. This often happens when you ask a *wh-* question with an auxiliary verb (*do, did, have,* etc.) To express surprise in a *wh-* question, you can add the words "on earth" or "in the world" to your question. Be sure to use exclamation intonation. Here are some examples:

Long Form	Short Form
What did you do this weekend?	Whadja do this weekend?
What on earth did you do?!	What on earth didja do?!
How did your weekend go?	Howdjer weekend go?
Whom did you go with?	Whodja go with?
When did you go?	Whendja go?
Where did you go last weekend?	Wheredja go last weekend?
How have you been?	How've you been?
What have you been up to?	Whadaya been up to?

Pronunciation Note: Notice that the "y" (as in *you*) sounds like /dʒ/* when it follows the /d/ sound. Here are some examples:

Long Form	Short Form
did you	didja
could you	couldja
would you	wouldja

Note: /dʒ/ is pronounced as *j*.

C. Practice. Audio   Listen to this short conversation. You'll hear the reduced forms of some words. Fill in the blanks with the long forms.

A: Hi, Sarah. _____ do this weekend?

B: Hi, David. I went to the beach.

A: _____ go?

B: On Sunday.

A: _____ go?

B: To Mariner Point. It was great.

A: Wow. _____ go with?

B: Jeff.

A: _____ go surfing?

B: No, it was too cold to go in the water, so we just sat on the sand and talked.

The Voiced /ð/ Sound Audio

The voiced /ð/ sounds the same as /d/ to some students and /z/ to others, but they are pronounced differently. Listen to these contrasts:

/d/	/z/	/ð/
den	Zen	then
breeding	breezing	breathing
bade	bays	bathe

Note: The IPA (International Phonetic Alphabet) symbol for the voiced *th* sound is ð.

D. Practice. Audio   In each pair of words, circle the one that you hear.

1. Zen   then   6. wordy   worthy

2. breeding   breathing   7. closing   clothing

3. bays   bathe   8. dough   though

4. Dan   than   9. Dave   they've

5. day   they   10. load   loathe

E. Practice. Audio   Look again at the box on this page. Repeat the words after the speaker.

F. Practice. Audio   Read along as you listen to these short conversations. Then listen again and repeat each sentence after the speaker. Pay special attention to words with the voiced /ð/.

1. A: So there's a problem with my essay?

   B: Well, it's a little wordy. It wouldn't be hard to shorten it, though.

2. A: This work really isn't worthy of them.

   B: I agree. They've done much better than this before.

3. A: I just heard that my favorite clothing store is closing for good!

   B: You mean Then Zen is going out of business? Good! It was always much too expensive. I never dared to go there.

Review: Language Functions

Making Small Talk with Friends

Listen to these examples of starting a conversation. You'll use this function in the next section.

Put It Together

Starting a Conversation. **Pair**   Start a conversation with a classmate by asking a question about what he or she has been doing lately. When your partner answers, ask another related question. Make sure that your question intonation is correct. If you'd like, try to use natural pronunciation of words that are often reduced. Exchange roles and have another brief conversation.

. : : : : : **Part Four** Broadcast English: Anthology
of African American Literature

Before Listening

A. Predicting. **Pair**   You're going to listen to a radio interview about a new **anthology**—collection—of African American literature. Before you listen to the interview, brainstorm your answers to this question and write them in the blanks.

• If you were putting together an anthology of the best literature of any group of people, what *kinds* of literature would you include (e.g., short stories)?

_____   _____

_____   _____

_____   _____

B. Thinking Ahead. **Pair**   Take a few minutes and consider by yourself what specific pieces of literature you might include in an anthology of *your* culture. In other words, what represents the best of your literary tradition? List at least three pieces of literature and tell your partner why these are important to include in your anthology.

C. Vocabulary Preparation.   There are words and expressions in the radio interview that may be new to you. First, read each sentence and guess the meaning of the underlined words. Then choose their meaning from the definitions in the box. Write the letters in the blanks.

Sentences

_____   1. Dr. Martin Luther King, Jr. was a religious leader who was famous for his extraordinary speaking ability. When he gave the <u>sermon</u> on Sundays, people felt transformed by his persuasive words.

_____   2. Her children grew up to be responsible, loving, happy, successful adults. They are <u>a testament to</u> her good parenting skills.

_____   3. Music by dozens of the best African American singers and musicians—Duke Ellington, Count Basey, and Sarah Vaughn, to name a few—are brought together <u>under one roof</u> on this one marvelous CD.

_____   4. I want to <u>refute</u> his stereotype of my culture. He has such an ignorant image of people from my country!

_____   5. My brother has a pretty good collection of blues music, but he also has a lot of rap—which drives me crazy—and he doesn't have any <u>spirituals</u> at all.

_____   6. <u>By and large</u>, the market for rap music consists of young people.

_____   7. Her writing was the <u>benchmark</u> in her field. Everyone else has to work extra hard to achieve the same quality.

_____   8. John has a technique for working on group projects with his classmates; he divides the project into sections that each person can complete <u>discretely</u>, and then at the end he puts all the parts together.

_____   9. We have occasional <u>tussles</u> over what kind of music to play. Claire likes rap, but I prefer jazz.

_____   10. When she wants to play rap and I want jazz, sometimes we <u>compromise</u> and put on some New Age music.

_____   11. There's an entire <u>genre</u> of literature based on the immigrant experience.

_____   12. The level of <u>literacy</u> is quite high. Almost 98 percent of the population has gone to school.

Definitions

a. in the same place

b. the ability to read and write

c. religious songs

d. arguments

e. lecture or talk that is given during a church service

f. category; type

g. mostly

h. prove to be wrong

i. separately

j. evidence of

k. standard by which others are judged

l. settle an argument by agreeing on something in the middle

Listening

A. Listening for the Main Idea. **Audio** As you listen to the interview the first time, try to answer this question:

- What types of literature are included in the *Norton Anthology of African American Literature?*

When you finish listening, write as many as you can remember.

_____   _____   _____

_____   _____   _____

_____   _____   _____

_____   _____   _____

B. Listening for Reasons. **Audio** Listen again to short pieces of the interview. Write your answers to the following questions. Write just phrases, not complete sentences.

1. Why did the editors create this anthology? _____

_____

2. Why was it so difficult to decide which contemporary authors to include? _____

_____

C. Listening for Details. **Audio** Read over these questions. Write brief answers to some of them now. Then listen again to the interview and answer the rest of the questions.

1. What is the first section of the anthology?

_____

2. Who was the market for black music?

_____

3. Who was the market for black literature?

_____

4. What were some arguments that the editors had over what to include in the anthology?

_____

5. What was unique about the African American slaves?

_____

6. What is one of the fundamental themes of the anthology?

_____

listening Strategy

Guessing Meaning from Context (Audio)

Speakers often say something in several different ways. They may restate a phrase or use a synonym for a word in an attempt to better communicate, to be clear. Your understanding of spoken English will improve if you listen for such restatements instead of focusing on the words that you don't know.

D. Guessing Meaning from Context. (Audio)   Listen to these words in the context of sentences from the interview. Write the meanings in the blanks.

1. marvelous = _____

2. canon = _____

3. sublime = _____

After Listening

Discussion. (Group)   Discuss the answers to these questions.

1. What types of literature are included in this anthology? (Ten are mentioned in the interview.) Are any of these surprising to find in an anthology of literature?

2. If *you* were editing an anthology of literature, what would you include? On the chart on page 123, put only pieces of literature that everyone in your group agrees on. Be sure to discuss *why* you've chosen each one. In other words, what does each represent? When you finish, compare your chart with those of other groups. Choose *one* of these options.

  • If everyone in your class is from the same culture, discuss what to include in an anthology of literature from your culture.

  • If students in your class are from different cultures, discuss what to include in an anthology of world literature.

Anthology of Literature	
Songs	
Folktales	
Poems	
Plays	
Short Stories	
Novels	

. : : : : Part Five Academic English: American Folk Heroes

Before Listening

A. Thinking Ahead. **Group**   You're going to listen to a lecture about American folk heroes and how they demonstrate unique aspects of U.S. culture. Before listening, discuss the answers to these questions.

1. Have you read Homer's *Iliad* or *Odyssey?* If so, share with your group something you remember about the heroes in these epics.

2. Who are some heroes in the folklore of your culture? Why are these heroes important in the culture? In other words, what do they represent or explain about your culture?

3. Name any American folk heroes that you already know about. These can be traditional characters from folk stories or folk songs, or they can be contemporary heroes from literature or films. What do you think these characters represent about U.S. culture?

B. Background Reading. ⬤Audio⬤   Before you listen to the lecture, read this version of a famous American folk story about Brer (Brother) Rabbit. You can also listen to it and follow along. Notice the southern accent. There are many stories about this rabbit and the other animals in his world—foxes, bears, dogs, racoons, and so on. In most of these tales, like the one that follows, Brer Rabbit—being smaller and weaker than the other animals—must **use his wits;** in other words, he has to be both quick and intelligent in order to survive in a dangerous world. Such stories were popular in the African American community in the southern United States long before they were written down in the nineteenth century by Joel Chandler Harris. As you read, think about the answer to the following question. You'll discuss this later, after the lecture.

- Why might this story have been important to African Americans in the early 1800s?

Brer Rabbit and the Briar Patch*

The day came when Brer Rabbit knew his fate was sealed; he was in terrible, inescapable trouble. His longtime enemy, Brer Fox, had caught him, tied him up,
5 and was planning to barbecue him for dinner. Brer Fox was gleefully hopping around with the anticipation of a meal of rabbit. Brer Rabbit knew he had to think fast.

"Brer Fox," he said to his captor in a sad,
10 pleading voice, "I don't care what you do with me, but just don't throw me into the briar patch. You can barbecue me, roast me, or boil me, but please don't fling me into the briar patch."

Brer Fox considered this.

15   "It's too much trouble to make a fire," Brer Fox said, "so I guess maybe I'll hang you."

"Hang me as high as you like," said Brer Rabbit. "That's fine with me. Just please, please don't fling me in the briar patch."

"Well," said Brer Fox, "I don't have any rope, so maybe I can drown you, instead."

"Drown me as deep as you like," said Brer Rabbit, "but please don't fling me in the
20 briar patch."

"There isn't any water around here," said Brer Fox, "so I guess I'll have to skin you."

"That's a good idea," said Brer Rabbit. "That's fine with me. Skin me, take out my eyes, cut off my ears, and cut off my legs, but please, *please* don't throw me in that briar patch."

*Note: A **briar patch** is an area with many, many dangerously thorny bushes (plants with sharp spikes, such as you see on a cactus)

Now Brer Fox had a serious decision to make. He wanted rabbit for dinner, but he hated
25 Brer Rabbit more than anything and wanted to hurt him as much as possible. He thought
about the possibilities. Then he picked up Brer Rabbit by his back legs and flung him far
into the middle of the briar patch.

Brer Fox waited a few minutes, expecting to hear sounds of terrible pain coming from
the briar patch. Instead, however, he heard some quiet noises in the bushes. Then he heard
30 somebody calling him. He looked up. There, on a hill on the other side of the briar patch,
sat Brer Rabbit, looking amazingly healthy and very pleased with himself.

"Don't you know?" he yelled to Brer Fox. "I was bred and born in the briar patch! Bred
and born! This here is my *home!*" With that, he hopped happily away, a free rabbit.

C. Thinking of Questions.   Before you listen to the lecture "American Folk Heroes," think of
questions that you think the speaker might answer. Write them in the blanks.

_____

_____

_____

_____

_____

 academic Strategy

Organizing Lecture Notes Graphically

It's good to be flexible about the *form* of your lecture notes. Sometimes an outline or modified outline
is the best form. Sometimes, as in Chapter Two, it's best to put some information on one side of a
vertical line and other information on the other side. In some classes, such as art history, you might
need to quickly draw figures that the professor shows on a screen and then add written notes next
to each one. For some lectures, a **graphic organizer** is the easiest and most logical form for your
notes.

Practice.   Look over the graphic organizer on pages 127–128. You'll use this to help you take notes
for the lecture in this chapter.

D. Using Abbreviations. In the box at the top of the graphic organizer on page 127 is a list of words that you'll hear often in the lecture. Decide on your own abbreviation for each one and write it there.

Listening

A. Vocabulary Preparation. (Audio) Listen to the following words in the context of sentences. Choose the meaning of each from the list. Put the letter of its meaning in the correct blank.

Words

_____ **1.** analogy

_____ **2.** saga

_____ **3.** prowess

_____ **4.** rambunctious

_____ **5.** exploits

_____ **6.** moral

_____ **7.** confront

_____ **8.** encroaching

_____ **9.** snobbish

_____ **10.** ignoble

_____ **11.** manipulate

_____ **12.** elitism

Meanings

a. a long adventure story with a hero

b. dishonorable; having or showing no honor, decency, or courage

c. similarity

d. courage; superior skills; also, heroism

e. with uncontrollable enthusiasm; lacking in discipline

f. the practical lesson of a story

g. advancing step by step beyond the usual limits

h. belief in the superiority of one's social class

i. acting proud and superior (especially to people of a lower social class)

j. manage or control for one's own purpose

k. encounter; face (or meet) a challenging situation

l. heroic acts

B. Listening for Main Ideas. (Audio) Listen once to the entire lecture. (You'll listen again later.) As you listen this time, don't take notes. Instead, follow along with the graphic organizer and keep these questions in mind:

• Who are five American folk heroes?

• What can you learn about American culture from stories about each one?

Key

Words in the Lecture	My Abbreviations	Words in the Lecture	My Abbreviations
hero(es)	_____	geological formation(s)	_____
social/society	_____	exploit(s)	_____
economic	_____	technology	_____
opportunity(-ies)	_____	confront	_____
natural phenomena	_____	individualism	_____

American Folk Heroes

Folk heroes = _heroes that slowly evolved and cannot be identified_
_____ _with a particular author_

Am. situation: _____

_____

Hero: _____

Info abt him:	Represents/Reflects:	Exploits explain:

_____   _____   _____

_____   _____   _____

_____

Hero: _____

Info abt him:	Exploits explain/show:

_____   _____

_____   _____

Hero: _____

Info abt him: Represents:

_____   _____

_____   _____

_____   _____

Hero: _____

Info abt him: Symbolizes/Represents:

_____   _____

_____   _____

_____   _____

_____   _____

Hero: _____

Info abt him: Story focuses on:

_____   _____

_____   _____

_____   _____

_____   _____

Concl./Review

Heroes: Represent/Mean:

_____   _____

_____   _____

_____   _____

_____   _____

All of these heroes _____

listening Strategy

Finding a Synopsis in the Conclusion to a Lecture Audio

A well-organized speaker often gives students a **synopsis** of the speech or lecture in its conclusion. In other words, the lecturer uses the conclusion to restate, or to review, the main ideas. This gives you the opportunity to hear the main points again, in slightly different words.

If you have a cassette recording of a professor's lecture, you can listen again at home, fill in any details missing from your notes, and use a well-organized conclusion to help you review for an exam.

Important note: Before recording any professor's lecture, *be sure to ask that professor for permission.*

C. Practice. Audio Before you listen to the entire lecture again, listen to just the ending and fill in as much as you can of the Conclusion/Review on page 128.

D. Taking Notes. Audio Listen to the entire lecture again. This time take notes to complete the graphic organizer.

E. Checking Your Understanding. Answer as much of this question as you can, either from memory or from your notes. After you answer, go on to Exercise F if you have missing information.

- Who are five American folk heroes, and what can you learn about American culture from stories about them?

F. (Optional) Filling in the Gaps. Audio Listen one last time to the entire lecture and fill in any gaps in your graphic organizer.

After Listening

academic Strategy

Comparing Lecture Notes

Most students find it helpful to join a study group (such as the one you saw in Part Two of Chapter One) with several other students in the same class. In a study session, you can compare your lecture notes with those of other students, fill in any information that you missed, and correct anything that you misunderstood.

Practice. Compare the notes on your graphic organizer with those of two or three other students. Add or correct anything that you need to.

A. Predicting Exam Questions. **Group**   What questions might a professor ask on an exam based on the lecture "American Folk Heroes"? Brainstorm for several short-answer questions (i.e., questions that can be answered in a sentence or two) and several essay questions (i.e., questions to be answered in one or more paragraphs). Write your questions in the blanks.

Examples: What are folk heroes, and how are they created?

What is the implicit moral of American tall tales such as "Pecos Bill" and "Paul Bunyan"?

_____

_____

_____

_____

_____

B. Discussion. **Pair**   Discuss the answers to these questions about the lecture.

1. What information in the lecture **confirmed** (supported) what you already knew about American culture?

2. What new information in the lecture surprised or interested you?

 Step Beyond

A. Choosing a Topic.   You're going to give a presentation to either a small group or the whole class. (Your teacher will decide which.) Choose *one* of the following topics:

• a folktale from your culture that explains a natural phenomenon or geological formation

• a folktale from your culture with a hero who exemplifies the ideal personal characteristics in the culture

• a folktale from your culture that includes a moral at the end

• a folktale from your country with a hero who expresses the unique history or culture of a minority group

B. Preparing Your Presentation. Follow these steps to prepare for your presentation.

1. Think through the entire story.

2. Put key actions or points of the story on index cards, in note form. Do not write out the whole story.

3. Look up any words that you need but don't already know in English.

4. Include in your notes any explanations that your audience might need. (For example, in the story about Shine, the listeners might need to know that a "coal shoveler" is a person who moves coal into a furnace for fuel.)

5. Now make notes of analysis of your folktale. In other words, prepare to tell your listeners what this story expresses about your culture or country.

C. Giving Your Presentation. Follow these steps as you give your presentation.

1. As you're telling your folktale, don't read from your notes. Instead, just glance at them occasionally if you need to jog your memory. Try to relax and enjoy telling the story.

2. After you've told your folktale, pause for a few seconds before giving your analysis, to signal the end of the story.

3. Keep your analysis short and focused. Your analysis shouldn't attempt to include the entire history or social structure of your people!

4. At the end, ask your listeners if they have any questions.

D. Responding to a Presentation. Be prepared, in case there is time to do so, either to ask a question or to tell the speaker what you enjoyed about the presentation.

chapter Five

Developing Nations

In this chapter, you'll read about how microcredit has helped poor women. You'll listen to information about economic problems in developing countries and discuss possible solutions to these problems.

. : : ┊ ┊ **Part One** Introduction: Moving Out of Poverty

A. Thinking Ahead. (Group)   Discuss the answers to these questions.

1. What does it mean to be poor? What does it mean to be wealthy?

2. How do economists define these terms? What are some other ways of defining these terms?

3. What basic items does every person need to live a good life? Why is it difficult for many people to acquire these things? Is it possible for all people to have these basic things? Why or why not?

B. Reading.   One solution to the problem of poverty is microcredit. Microcredit refers to programs that give small loans to very poor people for self-employment projects. The money that they earn from their businesses helps them care for themselves and their families. Read the following excerpts from the Microcredit Summit's website about three women who have changed their lives and moved out of poverty, thanks to microcredit loans.

Microcredit Success Stories

Nurjahan

Nurjahan is a borrower of the Grameen [microcredit] Bank in Bangladesh. Her name means "the light of the world." Nurjahan was abandoned by her parents at three months of age and raised by a neighbor. She was married at twelve, but her husband left her a year later. She was three months preg-
5 nant at the time. She returned to the family who had raised her, and cooked for them while she raised her son.

  Before she joined Grameen, Nurjahan had never earned more than $37.50 in a year and owned no land. After five years as a borrower with the Grameen Bank, her annual income is $250 (just above the national average) and she owns two goats, one
10 pregnant cow, ten hens, and two-thirds of an acre of land. The land cost $1,000, more than four times the average annual income. Seasonally, she employs two farm hands to assist with her rice crop. In a country where only 46 percent of the children reach grade five, Nurjahan's son is now in eighth grade.

La Maman Mole Motuke

La Maman Mole Motuke lived in a wrecked car in a suburb of Kinshasa, Zaire, with her four children. If she could find something to eat, she would feed two of her children; the next time she found something to
20 eat, her other two children would eat.

When organizers from the Association [a microcredit bank] interviewed her, she said that she knew how to make *chikwangue* (a Zairean food item), and she only needed a few dollars to start production.
25 After six months of training in marketing and production techniques, Maman Motuke got her first loan of US$100 [one hundred dollars in U.S. money], and bought production materials.

Today, Maman Motuke and her family no longer live in a broken down car; they rent a house with two bedrooms and a living room. Her four children go to school on a regular
30 basis; they eat regularly and dress well. She currently is saving money to buy some land in a suburb farther outside of the city and hopes to build a house.

Altagracia Damian

Altagracia Damian started a tiny ceramics business in the Dominican Republic. She believes that development, whether personal or professional, is the result of
35 human and economic resources. When she started her business in 1987, she had only 16 cents in her pocket.

After a few years of minimal operation, Altagracia went to ADEMI [a microcredit bank] for a loan. She received $80, which she used to purchase clay and
40 glazes. Since then, she has received a total of eight loans from ADEMI.

Although Altagracia doesn't pay herself a fixed salary, she now has seven employees working in her business. She says that thanks to the support of ADEMI, she has been able to climb out of extreme poverty and manage a growing business while paying for her
45 children's education.

Source: "Nurjahan," "La Maman Mole Motuke," and "Altagracia Damian" adapted from "Microcredit Success Stories" from Microcredit Summit. Available from www.microcreditsummit.org/stories/intro.htm; INTERNET. Reprinted with permission.

C. Vocabulary Check.   Find words in the reading passage that mean the following:

1. left by someone or something = _____

2. yearly = _____

3. an object that is destroyed and/or is not working = _____

4. objects made from baked clay = _____

5. valuable items that a person, an organization, or a country owns = _____

6. unchanging = _____

7. to leave a difficult situation = _____

D. Discussion. `Group`   Discuss the answers to these questions.

1. Most people who receive microcredit are women. How would you explain this fact?

2. What does Altagracia Damian mean by the following: "Development, whether personal or professional, is the result of human and economic resources"?

3. Compare microcredit loans to giving people welfare. What are the advantages and disadvantages of each?

E. Freewriting.   Choose *one* of these topics. Write about it for fifteen minutes. Don't worry about grammar and don't use a dictionary. Just put as many ideas as you can on paper.

- your reaction to the reading

- your ideas on microcredit loans compared to welfare. Which is better? Why?

- your ideas on other ways to solve the problem of poverty

. : : : : : **Part Two** Everyday English: Solutions to Poverty (Interview)

Before Listening

A. Predicting. `Group`   You are going to listen to Evan interview people on the street. He's going to ask them how to end poverty in the United States or in developing nations. Make predictions about what you will hear. What kinds of ideas do you think that most people will have? Do most people think that welfare is a good idea? What other solutions to poverty will people have?

B. Vocabulary Preparation.   You are going to hear the people in the interview use some words and expressions that may be new to you. First, read each sentence and guess the meaning of the underlined words. Then choose their meaning from the definitions in the box. Write the letters in the blanks.

Sentences

_____ **1.** I am going to <u>hand out</u> these assignments to everyone in the class.

_____ **2.** He is not <u>covered</u> by health insurance, so he has to pay for medical services with his own money.

_____ **3.** The government of Xenrovia does not provide enough of <u>a safety net</u> for its citizens; many working people would lose their savings if they had to pay for a serious medical problem.

_____ **4.** That country has an excellent <u>social welfare policy</u>: it provides free education, healthcare, and job training for all citizens.

_____ **5.** He said that he was <u>disadvantaged</u> as a child, but actually, he had a better home life and a better education than most children do.

Definitions
a. government services or money intended to take care of its citizens' basic needs
b. give; distribute
c. something that helps people when they are in a bad situation
d. protected
e. without money and other basic needs

Listening

A. Listening for the Main Idea. **(Video/Audio)**   Now listen to the interview. As you listen, try to answer this question:

• Do most people think that welfare is the solution to poverty?

listening Strategy

Managing a Conversation (Audio)

People often use words and expressions that do not have much meaning but serve an important purpose: conversation management. Conversation management terms have many uses. One is to give the speaker time to think of what he or she wants to say. These expressions tell the listener, "I'm not finished talking yet; I'm still thinking." It's a good idea to recognize these when you are speaking to someone so that you know when he or she needs time to think. Here are some examples:

More Formal

- again
- in terms of
- as I say/said
- I mean
- well
- uh (or um)
- you know
- kind of
- like

Less Formal

B. Listening to Conversation Management Expressions. (Video/Audio)   Listen again to some of the people from the interview. Listen for conversation management expressions. When you hear one of these expressions, write it in the blank.

1. **Speaker 1:** _____, I think that they should do something to, _____, give them some jobs not just give them money, _____.

2. **Speaker 2:** I think the most important thing is—rather than create government programs that just hand out money and welfare programs—the best thing to do is to increase education opportunities for, _____, those who've been, _____, disadvantaged in the past.

3. **Speaker 7:** _____, that's a question that you just can't answer unless you study a lot of economics and social sciences.

C. Listening for Details. Video/Audio   Listen to part of the interview again. This time, fill in the chart with the following information about each speaker that you hear: Does the speaker have a solution to the problem of poverty? Circle *yes* or *no* in the appropriate column.

Then listen again. This time, listen for the answer to this question: If the speaker has a solution, is the solution welfare? Or does he or she have other ideas? Take notes on his or her suggestions in the appropriate blanks.

Speaker Number	Does He or She Have a Solution?	Welfare/Other
1	Yes No	jobs
2	Yes No	
3	Yes No	
4	Yes No	

listening Strategy

Guessing the Meaning of Proverbs from Context Audio

Every language has proverbs—well-known sayings that express some wisdom about life. If you hear a proverb that is new to you, you can sometimes guess its meaning from context. Here is an example:

> This class is very popular, so I recommend that you register soon. Remember, <u>the early bird catches the worm</u>.

You can guess this proverb means that if you are competing with others for something desirable, you have a better chance of success if you act as quickly as possible.

D. Guessing the Meaning of Proverbs from Context. [Video/Audio]   Listen to a part of the interview again. Guess the meaning of the following proverb by paying attention to its context. Write your guess in the blanks.

"Give a man a fish, he'll eat for a day. Teach a man to fish, he'll eat for a lifetime."

_____

_____

_____

After Listening

A. Taking a Survey. [Group]   You are going to interview three students in your class about their solutions to the problem of poverty. Write their suggestions in the chart.

Student Name	Student 1 _____	Student 2 _____	Student 3 _____
1. What should we do to end poverty in the United States?			
2. Do you have the same solutions for other nations? If not, what are your suggestions?			
3. Is welfare the answer to the problem of poverty? Why or why not?			
4. Write your own question on the topic of solutions to poverty. _____ _____			

B. Discussing Survey Results. [Group]   Form small groups. Try not to be in a group with someone that you interviewed. Discuss the results of your survey. Did any of the advice surprise you? Were there any unusual suggestions?

. : : : : : **Part Three** The Mechanics of Listening and Speaking

Intonation

Tone of Voice That Changes Meaning (Audio)

Several interjections in English are common in conversation and carry meaning. Here are some examples:

Interjections	Meanings
Uh-huh.	Yes.
Uh-huh.*	You're welcome.
Uh-huh!	Yes!
Uh-uh.	No.
Uh-oh.	There's trouble/a problem.

*Because this has two different meanings, you can understand the meaning only from the context.

As you see, you can express meaning with more than words. Tone of voice can completely change the meaning of a word or phrase. Here are some examples:

Word or Phrase	Meanings
Yeah.	Yes.
Yeah!	I really agree!
Yeah?	Really? OR: Is that true?
Yeah . . .	I don't think so . . .
Come on!	Please!
Come on.	You're not serious. (indicates sarcasm)
Yeah, right.	You're right. OR: I agree.
Yeah, right.	You're wrong. OR: I disagree. (indicates sarcasm)

A. Practice. (Audio)   Listen to each conversation. What does the second person mean? Circle the letter of the answer.

1. *a.* Yes.
   b. No.
   c. You're welcome.
   d. There's trouble.
   e. I really agree!

2. *a.* Yes.
   b. No.
   c. You're welcome.
   d. There's trouble.
   e. I really agree!

3. *a.* Yes.
   b. I really agree!
   c. Really?
   d. I don't think so . . .
   e. You're not serious.

4. *a.* Yes.
   b. No.
   c. You're welcome.
   d. There's trouble.
   e. I really agree!

5. *a.* Yes.
   b. I really agree!
   c. Really?
   d. I don't think so . . .
   e. You're not serious.

6. *a.* Yes.
   b. I really agree!
   c. Really?
   d. I don't think so . . .
   e. You're wrong.

Language Function

Giving Advice and Suggestions in the Present (Audio)

To give advice, use the modals *should* or *ought to* + the simple form of a verb. You can give advice to another person (*you, he, she, they*) or to yourself (*I, we*). Here is an example:

Q: So what do you think I <u>should do</u> about this economics class?

A: I think you <u>ought to join</u> a study group.

Should and *ought to** mean "it's a good idea."

To express "it's not a good idea," use *shouldn't* + the simple form of the verb. Here is an example:

I think you <u>shouldn't worry</u> about it.

*__Ought to__ isn't used very often in the negative form.

Similar to advice, suggestions are given when you want to be helpful. They're less forceful than advice. Use *can, could, might,* or *Why don't you . . .?* to make suggestions. Here are some examples:

Suggestions: You <u>might join</u> a study group.   **Less Forceful**

                You <u>could join</u> a study group.

                Well, you <u>can join</u> a study group.

                <u>Why don't you join</u> a study group?**

Advice: You <u>should</u> join a study group.

                You <u>ought to</u> join a study group.   **More Forceful**

You can make advice even stronger by adding <u>really</u> before <u>ought to</u> or <u>should</u>. Here is an example:

    You <u>really ought to</u> join a study group.

**This seems like a question but is usually, in fact, a suggestion. Use this structure only with *I, you,* or *we.*

B. Practice. **Audio**   Listen to Speaker A's problem. Use the cues to give present advice or suggestions to Speaker A.

Example: ask/teacher

          A: I don't understand these economics terms.

          B: Why don't you ask the teacher?

1. (go/library) B: _____

2. (start/now) B: _____

3. (do/more research) B: _____

4. (study/with me tonight) B: _____

5. (look for/his biography on the Web) B: _____

Language Function

Giving Advice and Suggestions for a Past Time **Audio**

Often, people give advice for a past time, when it's too late, and when the advice can't really be of any help. In such a case, use *should have* or *ought to have* + the past participle of the verb. Here are some examples:

Q: What do you think <u>we should have done</u>?

A: We <u>should have started</u> this term paper earlier.

   OR:

A: We <u>ought to have started</u> this earlier.

To give negative advice* for a past time, use *shouldn't have* + the past participle. Here is an example:

   We <u>shouldn't have waited</u> so long to get started on this.

Ought to isn't used very often in the negative past form, either.

C. Practice. **Audio**   Listen to Speaker A's problem. Use the cues to give past advice or suggestions to Speaker A.

Example: start/earlier

        A: We only have a few hours to prepare this presentation.

        B: We should have started earlier.

1. (be/more careful) B: _____

2. (use/more sources) B: _____

3. (ask/the T. A. to explain it) B: _____

4. (study/harder) B: _____

5. (budget/your money better) B: _____

Pronunciation

Reduced Forms in Expressions for Giving Advice and Suggestions (Audio)

When people speak quickly, some words become reduced, or short. Here are some examples of reductions in expressions for giving advice and suggestions:

Long Form	Short Form
We <u>ought to</u> do it.	We <u>otta</u> do it.
Why <u>don't you</u> do it?	Why <u>doncha</u> do it?
He <u>should have</u> done it.	He <u>shud uv</u> done it.
	OR:
	He <u>shudda</u> done it.
You <u>ought to have</u> done it.	You <u>otto uv</u> done it.
We <u>shouldn't have</u> done it.	We <u>shudden uv</u> done it.
	OR:
	We <u>shuddena</u> done it.

D. Practice. (Audio)   People say short forms but write the long forms. Listen to the following sentences and write the long form of the words you hear.

1. They _____ build the factory here.

2. They _____ built the factory there.

3. Why _____ take that class?

4. The government _____ started a microcredit program.

5. The government _____ started a microcredit program.

6. They _____ raised taxes.

Review: Language Functions

Giving Advice and Suggestions `Video/Audio`

Listen again to these examples of giving advice and suggestions. Pay attention to the intonation of giving advice and suggestions. You'll use these functions in the next section.

Put It Together

A. Practice. `Pair` Work with a partner. Person A will give advice or a suggestion. Person B will respond with an appropriate interjection or short expression.

Example: A: We should do this project together.

B: Yeah.

Person A thinks it would be good	Person B
1. to go to the library	agrees
2. for Person B to take a few more classes	expresses sarcasm
3. to take a survey and get students' opinions before doing their class presentation	strongly agrees
4. if Person B had bought a new computer	is hesitant; doesn't really agree
5. for Person B to buy some shares of IBM	indicates "no"

B. Practice. (Pair) Now exchange roles. (Person A becomes B, and B becomes A.) Continue as you did in Exercise A.

Person A thinks it would be good	Person B
1. to plan a class party	strongly agrees
2. to hire a five-piece band to play live music	indicates "no"
3. for Person B to do all of the cooking for it	expresses sarcasm
4. if you had done this sooner	agrees
5. to have the party at Person B's house	remembers that the house is very, very messy

. . : : : : : **Part Four** Broadcast English: Eradicating World Poverty

Before Listening

A. Thinking Ahead. (Group) You're going to listen to part of a radio interview with the director of the United Nations Development Program (or UNDP), Alan Doss, about his ideas on how to **eradicate** (completely eliminate) world poverty. In order to prepare for the program, discuss the following question.

• Is it possible to completely eradicate world poverty? If so, how? If not, why not?

B. Vocabulary Preparation.   There are words in the radio interview that may be new to you. First, read each sentence and guess the meaning of the underlined words. Then choose their meaning from the definitions in the box. Write the letters in the blanks.

Definitions

a. free food, clothing, or money   e. is the decision of

b. keep alive   f. give power to

c. state of not being equal   g. evidence; the outward sign of a condition

d. explain as the cause   h. removal of government control over business

---

Sentences

_____ 1. According to Alan Doss, if governments <u>empower</u> people, they will have the ability to eradicate poverty themselves.

_____ 2. The notion of charity as a way to help poor people is a bad idea, according to some people. Just giving people <u>handouts</u> won't help them succeed over time.

_____ 3. Five hundred calories a day is not enough to <u>sustain</u> an adult. You need at least 1,500 to have enough energy to work and remain healthy.

_____ 4. There's a growing <u>disparity</u> between the very rich of the world and the very poor. The rich are getting richer, and the poor are getting poorer.

_____ 5. In the past, experts have been treating the <u>manifestations</u> of poverty, such as hunger, rather than the causes.

_____ 6. Some experts <u>attribute</u> the decline in poverty in some parts of the world to an increase in trade. Others say that government programs in those countries have improved the situation.

_____ 7. Government policies have improved some countries' economic situations. For example, <u>deregulation</u> has stimulated trade in many developing nations.

_____ 8. According to Alan Doss, improving a country's economic situation <u>is up to</u> the government of that country.

Listening

A. Listening for the Main Idea. `Audio` Listen to the radio interview. As you listen, try to answer this question:

- How can countries eradicate poverty in twenty years, according to the UNDP?

 *listening* **Strategy**

Listening for Supporting Statistics `Audio`

Speakers often make an assertion and follow it with statistics that support it. The statistics strengthen the speaker's argument and make it more believable. Here are some examples:

Assertion: Poverty has been eradicated in Xenrovia.

Supporting Statistics:

- For one thing, unemployment is no longer a problem. We've seen the unemployment rate go from 9 percent to 4 percent in just five years.
- Another sign is the increase in income: There's been a 7 percent increase in the salary of the average worker since 1998.

B. Listening for Supporting Statistics. `Audio` Listen to the following segments of the interview. Write the statistics that support the speaker's assertions as you listen.

1. That's an important definition—the so-called "income definition" of poverty, and it shows up some very, very disturbing trends and facts. Uh, I think you'll have seen in the report that we estimate something like _____ billion people around the world live on less than _____ U.S. dollar a day. _____ of those people simply do not get enough calories every day to sustain a normal level of human activity. So poverty is important to talk about in income terms.

2. What has happened is that there is a growing disparity between the top and the bottom. On a worldwide scale, it's quite extraordinary what's happened in the last three decades. The ratio of the top _____ who—in terms of the percentage of wealth that they own, if you can put it that way—to the poorest _____—has gone from _____ to _____ to _____ to _____.

3. In the last fifty years, we have done more as a world community to lift people out of poverty
than we've done in the previous 500 years. Take the case of Malaysia. Twenty years ago it was
estimated that something close to _____ of Malaysia's people were living below
the poverty line. Today that's about _____.

academic Strategy

Understanding Latin Terms Audio

People often use Latin terms (and terms that come from Latin) in formal speaking situations. The
more you hear them, the better you'll understand them. Once you are comfortable with them, using
them in academic speaking situations can make you sound more fluent. Here are some common Latin
terms:

Latin Terms	Meanings
a priori	before the fact
ad hoc	for this purpose
ad nauseam	to the point of nausea; repeatedly; endlessly
modus operandi	way of doing something; method of procedure
per se	by itself
pro forma	made or done in a routine manner
quid pro quo	this for that (you do something for me, and I'll do something for you)
verbatim	word for word; literally

Practice.   Listen to the following sentences. Each has a Latin term. For each sentence, write the
correct meaning of the Latin term that you hear. Make your choices from the preceding list.

1. _____

2. _____

3. _____

4. _____

5. _____

C. Understanding Latin Terms.   Audio   Listen to a part of the program. The speaker uses a Latin term. Complete the following paraphrase of the speaker's statement by translating the Latin term.

What he's saying is that giving people money isn't the answer to poverty _____

_____

D. Guessing the Meaning of a Proverb from Context.   Audio   Review the information on proverbs that you read on page 141. Then listen to a part of the interview again. Guess the meaning of the following proverb by paying attention to its context. Write your guess in the blanks.

The rising tide lifts all boats: _____

_____

E. Listening for Details.   Audio   Listen again to part of the program. Listen for the answers to the following questions. Write your answers in the blanks.

A Chinese family enjoying high standards in education and health

1. Where in the world does poverty exist, according to the program? _____

_____

2. Is charity the answer to poverty, according to Doss? _____

_____

3. What is the solution to poverty, according to Doss? _____

_____

4. How else do you define poverty, besides according to income? _____

_____

5. Is poverty a problem in the United States? _____

After Listening

A. Discussion. **Group**   Discuss the answers to these questions.

1. How does Doss say that poverty can be eradicated in twenty years? Do you agree with him?

2. How have countries like Malaysia made economic progress?

3. Mary Ambrose says to Alan Doss: "One of the extraordinary images out of the report for me was the idea that if you took the world's seven richest men, you could provide basic social services for the entire world." Does this surprise you as well? Who are these people? If you could speak to them, what would you say? Would you try to convince them to share their wealth? Why or why not?

B. (Optional) Applying Your Knowledge.   Look around the community that you live in. Look for signs of great wealth and great poverty. What are the manifestations of wealth and poverty in your community? How wide is the gap between these two groups? Make notes on your observations and then share them with the class.

. . : : : **Part Five** Academic English: Amartya Sen and Development Economics

Before Listening

A. Brainstorming. **Group**   You are going to listen to a lecture about Amartya Sen, the 1998 recipient of the Nobel Prize for Economics. Sen looks at famine as one of the most extreme forms of poverty. Before you listen to the lecture, discuss what you know about famines: What causes them? Where have famines occurred in recent history?

Amartya Sen

B. Thinking Ahead.

1. Look at the picture on page 156 and the outline for the lecture on pages 157–159. What questions do you expect (or want) the speaker to answer? Is there anything that you're curious about? Write your questions in the blanks.

_____

_____

_____

_____

2. Now look over the questions in the Comprehension Check on page 161. Are any of these similar to your own questions?

C. Guessing Meaning from Context.
Guess the meanings of some of the words from the lecture. The words are underlined in the sentences. Look for clues to their meanings in the words around them.
   Write your guess in the blank after each sentence. Compare your answers with a partner's. Then check your guess with your teacher or the dictionary.

1. Although he was born in a developing nation, he came from a well-to-do family and always had adequate food, clothing, and educational opportunities.

   Guess: _____

2. Three million people starved to death in the famine that occurred in Calcutta in 1943.

   Guess: _____

3. There was no rain for six months last year. This led to a serious drought that killed all the crops.

   Guess: _____

4. Another year, the rain was so heavy that floods washed away the crops.

   Guess: _____

5. North Korea is an example of a country with an authoritarian regime: Only one person (or a few people) have absolute power, and the citizens have little or none.

   Guess: _____

6. When there were food shortages, many people <u>hoarded</u> food: They bought all they could, and the market shelves were empty in a very short time. This only made the shortage situation worse.

   Guess: _____

7. In order to <u>avert</u> a food shortage next time, the government is trying to educate people not to hoard.

   Guess: _____

8. If resources were distributed among all the citizens <u>equitably</u>, then everyone would have the same amount and no one would be without food.

   Guess: _____

9. The <u>gross domestic product</u> (GDP) of a country represents the value of all the goods and services that the country produces, but it's not a good indicator of how rich or poor the citizens of a country are, according to Amartya Sen.

   Guess: _____

Listening

A. Listening for the Main Idea. (Audio) You'll hear a
lecture called "Amartya Sen and Development Economics." Listen once to the entire lecture. (You'll listen again later.) As you listen this time, don't take notes. Instead, follow along with the outline and keep this question in mind:

• According to Amartya Sen, what causes famines?

Famine in Ethiopia

listening Strategy

Listening for Digressions `Audio`

Sometimes lecturers seem to go away from the lecture topic. Often they are adding information to or expanding on the topic, or simply helping you, the listener, think. However, what they say doesn't always fit neatly into the logical flow of the lecture. This may be important information, though, and you should probably note it down. One way to do this is to write the additional information in the margin of your notes. Lecturers often let you know when they are digressing by giving you certain cues. Some of these follow:

- Now, let's stop here for a second.
- By the way, . . .
- That reminds me . . .

Lecturers also often give you cues when they are returning to the main topic. Some examples of these include the following:

- Anyway, . . .
- Getting back to the subject . . .
- Now, let's return to . . .

B. Taking Notes. `Audio`   Listen to the lecture again. This time fill in the outline. As you listen, note places where the lecturer digresses, and try to record information from the digressions in the boxes provided. Note: Don't worry about the blanks labeled "supporting quotes" yet.

Amartya Sen and Development Economics

I. Amartya Sen

    A. Background: _Recipient of the Nobel Prize for Economics_____

    _____

> **Digression**
>
> Examples of famines in recent history: _____
>
> _____
>
> Traditional views on causes of famines: _____
>
> _____

    B. Area of specialization: _____

    _____

II. Beliefs About Famine

    A. Famine is *not* caused by _____

    B. Famine *is* caused by _____

    C. The situation in a democratic country: _____

        _____

    D. The situation in a country with an authoritarian regime: _____

        _____

        1. Who is affected in an authoritarian regime? _____

            _____

            Supporting quote: _____

            _____

        2. Example in Bangladesh: _____

            _____

    E. How to avert famine

        1. What won't work? Why not? _____

            _____

            _____

        2. What will work? Why? _____

Digression

The source for this information: _____

_____

        _____

        _____

    F. Summary statement: two underlying factors of all famines: _____

        _____

G. Why GDP is misleading: _____

_____

   Supporting quote: _____

_____

H. What is the "poverty index"? _____

_____

III. Conclusion

A. Acc. to Sen, taking care of the poor is _____

_____

B. Examples of societies that have high standards in education and health:

   1. China surpasses _____ because

   _____

   2. Costa Rica is a good ex. because _____

   3. _____

      a. Life expectancy: _____

      _____

      b. HDI (means: _____)

         rating:

      _____

C. Summary statement: When society takes care of most vulnerable, not only

   _____

   but _____

   _____

listening **Strategy**

Listening for Quoted Material (Audio)

Speakers and writers use quoted material to support points that they are making. In print, we use quotation marks to indicate quoted material. Here is an example:

> Amartya Sen has said, "It is not a question of more or less government but what kind of government."

When speakers refer to quoted material, they often say "quote" at the beginning of a quoted statement, and "unquote" at the end. Here is an example:

> Amartya Sen has said, <u>quote</u>, "It is not a question of more or less government but what kind of government." <u>Unquote</u>.

If the speaker is quoting a short statement, he or she might say "quote unquote" together, at the beginning of the quoted material. Here is an example:

> In 1970, Amartya Sen published *Collective Choice and Social Welfare* in which he offered an answer to U.S. economist Kenneth Arrow's <u>quote unquote</u> "impossibility theorem."

C. Taking Detailed Notes. (Audio)   Listen to the entire lecture again. This time take notes to complete the outline. Listen for references to quoted material and take notes on it.

D. Checking Your Notes. (Audio)   See if you can answer the following questions from your notes. If not, listen again to the lecture. This time, add more information to your outline.

1. What was happening in India when Sen was growing up? _____

_____

2. Where were some famines in recent history? _____

_____

3. What are some traditional beliefs about the causes of famine? _____

_____

4. If you wanted to read the original article to which the lecturer refers that discusses Sen's ideas

on averting famines, what publication would you look for? _____

_____

5. Who *doesn't* suffer when there is a famine in a dictatorial society, according to Sen? _____

_____

6. Why is it a mistake for economists to use GDP as an indicator of poverty, according to Sen?

_____

_____

7. What does Sen's "poverty index" refer to? _____

_____

E. Listening Again for Important Details. **Audio**   Go back to the beginning of Exercise D. Listen again to the parts of the lecture that answer the seven questions. Either check your answers or fill in missing answers.

F. (Optional) Filling in the Gaps. **Audio**   Listen one last time to the entire lecture and fill in any gaps in your outline.

After Listening

A. Comprehension Check.   Use your notes to write your answers to these questions. When you finish, compare your answers with a partner's.

1. What area of economics does Sen focus on? _____

2. What causes famine, according to Sen? _____

3. Why has famine been a problem in such countries as Somalia, Sudan, North Korea, China,

and India? _____

_____

4. Is growing more food the way to avert famine? _____

5. What is the answer to poverty, according to Sen? _____

6. What is Costa Rica a good example of? _____

B. Discussion. **Pair**   Discuss anything from the lecture that surprised you or interested you. Then make a list of everything that you've learned about development economics. (Try not to look back at your lecture notes.)

Step Beyond

A. Choosing a Topic.   You're going to give a 3–5 minute presentation to either a small group or the whole class. (Your teacher will decide which.) Choose *one* of the following projects.

Project 1

Find out if hunger is a problem in the community in which you live. If so, find out what people are doing to correct the problem and analyze these efforts. Are they effective? Why or why not?

Project 2

Find out more about microcredit. Who started it? Where and when did it start? How is it working today? What is its future?

Project 3

Do Web or library research to find out more about Amartya Sen's life. What was his career path? What stimulated his interest in development economics? What else does he do?

Project 4

Do Web or library research on the topic of famine. Find out as much as you can about famines throughout history. Choose one famine in particular and identify the country or government under which it occurred. Examine the country and the famine in light of Sen's ideas. Explain how the famine occurred and how it could have been avoided, according to Sen's economic theories.

B. Preparing Your Presentation.   Organize the notes you made on your research. Practice giving your presentation without looking at your notes. Make sure your presentation lasts only 3–5 minutes. Think of ways to make it interesting: Would pictures help? Photocopy some pictures from your sources and bring them to class.

speaking Strategy

Asking Questions After a Presentation

It's a good idea to ask a question after a presentation. Sometimes you'll have a question in mind before the presentation begins; other times, you'll think of one while you are listening. Keep a piece of paper nearby while you are listening to write down your question so you won't forget it when the time for questions comes. Asking questions after a presentation not only increases your knowledge on a subject, it also helps you pay attention and shows the speaker that you are interested in the subject.

C. Responding to a Presentation.   Be prepared, in case there is time to do so, either to ask a question or to tell the speaker what you enjoyed about the presentation.

chapter Six

The Global Economy

In this chapter, you'll read about a country with a transitional economy, Mongolia. You'll listen to information about and discuss how modernization and economic transition affect countries like Mongolia.

Part One Introduction: Election Day in Mongolia

Countries in Transition

Delivering
personal
computers
in Vietnam

Cellular phones in Thailand

Advertising Japanese cars in Myanmar

A. Thinking Ahead. **Pair**   Look at the photos on page 164. They show scenes from countries that have transitional economies, in other words, countries in transition from socialism to capitalism. Answer these questions.

1. What are some other countries with transitional economies?

2. What are some of the problems that countries in transition might face?

B. Reading.   Later in this chapter, you will hear a radio program about a country in transition: Mongolia. The former Soviet Union controlled Mongolia until 1991; now it has free elections and is slowly becoming a market economy. One new business in Mongolia is tourism. The following excerpt is from an article by an American who visited Mongolia as a tourist during an election. He describes a meeting with some Mongolian voters.

A four-year-old boy greets an American traveler in north central Mongolia.

Election Day in Mongolia

The voters, holding tightly onto their government identification booklets, stood close to the registrar, waiting their turn. This election was an important one for Mongolia. Until 1991, the country was part of the [former] Soviet Union. In the first free election after the collapse of the Soviet Union, the Commu-
5 nist Party had little opposition. It won 71 of 76 seats in the national parliament. But by 1995, new political parties had organized and were claiming more and more insistently that it was time for Mongolia to take a more open, capitalistic direction.

We walked outside into the bright sun. Men sat cross-
10 legged on the ground or leaned on their elbows, smoking pipes. The women sat talking in the shade. We sat down with five of the men and started asking
15 them questions. One man immediately assumed the role of elder statesman.

He took out a long, thin-stemmed pipe, carefully filled
20 the bowl with tobacco and adjusted the brim of his hat, casting a shadow over his eyes.

Facts about Mongolia
■ Population: About 2.3 million.
■ Geography: 604,000 square miles, about the size of Western Europe.
• Average elevation: more than 5,000 feet.
• Landscape ranges from high plains and alpine mountains to the massive Gobi Desert in the southern part of the country.
■ Economy: Half of the people are nomads, caring for 28 million sheep, goats, cattle, and horses.
• Exports are largely made up of minerals: molybdenum and copper.
Source: Chris Welsch. *Star Tribune:* August 4, 1996.

"Today's election is very important," he said, pointing at us with the pipe stem. "This year, there is a choice, and many people are coming to ask for what they want.
25 Last time, not so many people came. There weren't many choices."

He said he thought that about 80 percent of eligible voters would participate in the election. (It turned out to be more than 90.)

"What is it that you want?" Madin [the tour guide] asked.

"Most of us would like to have our own factories here," he said. "Canning fish
30 or cutting lumber. In a market economy, everyone will have their own things. There'll be less unemployment. Our country will make more contacts with other countries."

Through the interpreter, we asked the whole group questions, but only the smoker would speak. He said he was 55 years old, a herdsman with more than 50
35 sheep, along with some cattle, goats, and horses.

"What can foreigners do for us? What can you tell us?" he asked.

Madin said, "You can learn from our mistakes." He went on to explain how the American West was divided by fences, and that the nomadic lifestyle of the Mongolians would be threatened if the land was privatized. He talked about the prob-
40 lems caused by material greed in our country, about the wide gap between the very rich and the very poor.

I said I also wondered what might happen to Mongolia's traditional culture when modernization came. Material wealth often comes at the cost of traditional culture and values.

45   In those categories, Mongolia could have a lot to lose. Even after more than 70 years of repressive Communist rule, much of Mongolia's nomadic culture remains intact.

In these parts of Mongolia, there are no phones, no newspapers, and no roads. Horses are the primary mode of transportation. People still welcome travelers
50 because everyone is a traveler. Everyone relies on that hospitality; in one of the harshest climates in the world, it's more than courtesy. It's a matter of survival.

You don't have to knock on the door of a *ger* [a traditional nomadic home] in Mongolia. No one has to. It is polite just to walk into any stranger's home and sit down. The owners will immediately put water on the stove at the center of the *ger*
55 for tea and will share their food—probably yogurt, dried cheese, or fermented mare's milk.

The group listened to us talk about the pleasures and pains of life in America. And we listened to Madin explain how tourists like us would be coming in greater numbers to fish, ride horses, and enjoy the landscape, which, he explained, ap-
60 pealed to us because there are no telephone lines, concrete, or billboards.

The smoker paused to take it all in. "I understand that too much improvement can be a bad thing," he said without irony, puffing on his pipe.

Source: Chris Welsch, adapted from "Election Day in Mongolia" from *Star Tribune* (August 4, 1996). Reprinted with permission.

C. Vocabulary Check.   Find words and phrases in the reading passage that mean the following:

1. forcefully and without stopping = _____

2. took the [role] = _____

3. a politician = _____

4. a person who makes his living by raising sheep and cattle = _____

5. a lifestyle in which people follow their sheep and cattle around the country = _____

_____

6. a desire to have a lot more (money, etc.) than what is fair = _____

7. the use of words that are the opposite of what you mean = _____

D. Discussion. **Group**   Discuss the answers to these questions.

1. Do you agree with the advice that the American tour guide gave the herdsman? What advice would *you* give the herdsman?

2. What did the herdsman mean when he said, "I understand that too much improvement can be a bad thing"?

3. Can you think of examples of countries that have had "too much improvement"? What are they?

E. Freewriting.   Choose *one* of these topics. Write about it for fifteen minutes. Don't worry about grammar and don't use a dictionary. Just put as many ideas as you can on paper.

• your reaction to the reading

• your opinion of tourism in transitional countries: Is it good or bad? Why?

• examples of traditional cultures that have changed because of Western influences

. . : : : : **Part Two** Everyday English: Summer Jobs

Before Listening

A. Thinking Ahead. **Group**   You are going to hear Brandon, Jennifer, and Tanya talk about jobs. Before you listen, talk about jobs and career goals.

1. Have you chosen a career? If so, what is it? What are you doing to prepare for it?

2. Some students in the United States work during vacations to earn money for their college expenses. Do you ever work during school vacations? Why or why not? If you work during vacations, what kind of work do you find?

3. Some students also work during vacations to get experience in the field they are preparing for. These jobs are sometimes called internships. Have you ever had an internship? Have you ever had *any* job that was related to your career plans? If so, tell your group members about it.

B. Predicting.   In the conversation, the students talk about one way that some companies try to save money. How do companies try to save money?

C. Vocabulary Preparation: Informal Terms.   You are going to hear the students in the conversation use some expressions that are common in casual conversation. First, read each sentence on page 169 and guess the meaning of the underlined words. Then choose their meaning from the definitions in the box. Write the letters in the blanks.

Definitions
a. I have to leave right away! *d.* boring; unpleasant; unsatisfying
b. and everything; and things like that *e.* because
c. That sounds wonderful! *f.* What bad luck!

Sentences

_____ **1.** I don't want some <u>dumb</u> job this summer—I really want to do something interesting.

_____ **2.** I can't work this summer '<u>cause</u> I have to go to school.

_____ **3.** When Bill told me that he got a job at Macrosoft, I said, "<u>Cool!</u>"

_____ **4.** Tell me about your new job. Do you have your own office <u>an' all</u>?

_____ **5.** I heard you lost your job. <u>What a drag</u>!

_____ **6.** Class is starting in five minutes. <u>I'm outta here</u>!

Listening

A. Listening for the Main Idea. (Video/Audio) You're going to hear the students talk about jobs and goals. Listen to the entire conversation. As you listen, try to answer this question:

• What is Brandon's career goal?

B. Listening for Details. (Video/Audio) Listen again to the conversation. Then write your answers to these questions. Write short phrases, not complete sentences.

1. Why does Jennifer think Brandon is lucky?

_____

2. What kind of job did Brandon have last summer?

_____

3. Why is Brandon's company hiring programmers in Eastern Europe?

_____

4. How long has Brandon been working with computers?

_____

5. Why does Brandon say that he would hire cheap labor overseas?

_____

C. Listening for Inferences. (Video/Audio)   Listen again to short parts of the conversation. What can you infer from each? Circle the letter of the correct answer.

1. How do you think Tanya feels about the possibility of getting a good job this summer?

  a. optimistic; she thinks she has a good chance.

  b. pessimistic; she doesn't think she has a good chance.

  c. indifferent; she doesn't care.

  d. She doesn't have any idea of her chances.

2. How do you think Brandon feels about computer programming as a career goal?

  a. He's excited about it.

  b. He doesn't really want to do it anymore.

  c. He thinks he's too good to do it.

  d. He doesn't have an opinion.

3. How does Brandon's career goal compare to the kind of work that he's been doing since he was thirteen?

  a. It's about the same.

  b. It requires less responsibility.

  c. It requires more responsibility.

  d. It's in a totally different field.

4. Why might Jennifer think that Brandon's plan to hire cheap labor overseas for his company is a bad idea?

   a. The company loses money.

   b. It's bad for the economy of the country where the workers live.

   c. It's bad for U.S. citizens who need jobs.

   d. It makes products cost more.

5. Why might some people think Brandon's plan to hire cheap labor overseas for his company is a good idea?

   a. People who don't have a lot of money can buy his products.

   b. U.S. workers will have more jobs.

   c. He can give jobs to people who need them.

   d. It will make his products available overseas.

After Listening

A. Vocabulary Check: Workplace Terms. Pair   In the conversation, you heard some terms related to the workplace. Guess the meanings of some of the words from the conversation. The words are underlined in the sentences. Look for clues to their meanings in the words around them.

Write your guess in the blank after each sentence. Compare your answers with a partner's. Then check your guess with your teacher or the dictionary.

1. Macrosoft offered Monica a summer job <u>writing code</u>, but she's tired of computer programming.

   Guess: _____

2. Macrosoft offered her a job. It needed to replace some programmers because it had <u>let go</u> of several programmers.

   Guess: _____

3. Macrosoft thinks it can save money by <u>laying people off</u>.

   Guess: _____

4. Macrosoft also thinks it can save money by hiring <u>cheap labor</u> in Xenrovia.

   Guess: _____

5. I have a new business. In order to reduce costs and keep <u>overhead</u> low in the first few years, I'm not going to rent an office, buy a lot of equipment, or hire very many people.

Guess: _____

6. Macrosoft has a talented <u>workforce</u>—it hires only people who are highly trained and have a lot of experience.

Guess: _____

7. You don't have to actually work for Macrosoft; it's <u>contracting with</u> programmers just for this project.

Guess: _____

B. Taking a Survey. **Class**   Move around the classroom and interview other students. (In addition, for homework your teacher might have you interview other people in your school or neighborhood.) Ask people these questions.

• Is it a good idea for companies in a country such as the United States to hire cheap labor overseas? Why or why not?

Take notes on your survey using a chart like the one below. You may want to keep track (卌) of the people who say that it's a good idea and those who say that it isn't.

Survey Results	
Total number of people you asked: _____	
Total number of people who said it's a good idea: _____	Total number of people who said it's a bad idea: _____
Examples of reasons:	Examples of reasons:

C. Reporting Your Findings. **Pair**   Explain your survey results to a classmate.

·.·:·::·:: **Part Three** The Mechanics of Listening and Speaking

Language Functions

Asking for Confirmation `Audio`

Sometimes you say something based on information that you believe (or assume) is true. This is an assumption. But to be polite, you want the listener to **confirm** (or support) your assumption. To ask for confirmation, you can add a tag question to your statement, or you can add a separate question. Here are some examples:

- Brandon always seems to get a career-related summer job, doesn't he?
- You always get a career-related summer job, don't you, Brandon?
- You always get a career-related summer job, huh?
- Brandon always seems to get a career-related summer job. Isn't that so?

Offering an Explanation `Audio`

When someone makes an assumption about you, it may or may not be correct. If the speaker asks for confirmation, you have an opportunity to agree, disagree, correct, or explain the assumption. Here are some examples:

A: You always have good luck finding a career-related summer job, don't you, Brandon?

B: Well, I was lucky last summer. . . . (Agreement)

Not always. The summer before last I worked at the video store. (Disagreement)

I wouldn't call it luck . . . more like persistence. (Correction)

True, but I work pretty hard to find it. (Explanation)

A. Practice. `Audio`   Listen to this assumption. Then listen to different responses to the assumption. Decide if each response is agreement, disagreement, correction, or explanation. Check (✓) the answer.

Response	Agreement	Disagreement	Correction	Explanation
1				
2				
3				
4				
5				
6				

Intonation

Tag Question Intonation Audio

The intonation for a tag question depends on whether or not you are sure that your assumption is correct and that the listener will agree with you. If you are sure, you use falling intonation. Here is an example:

You always have good luck finding a career-related summer job, don't you, Brandon? (Sure.)

If you are *not* sure of your assumption and you're asking for a real answer from your listener, you use rising intonation. Here is an example:

You always have good luck finding a career-related summer job, don't you, Brandon? (Not sure.)

B. Practice. Audio   Listen to the following statements with tag questions. Decide whether the speaker is sure or not sure (and is asking for information). Circle your answer.

1. Sure   Not Sure   5. Sure   Not Sure

2. Sure   Not Sure   6. Sure   Not Sure

3. Sure   Not Sure   7. Sure   Not Sure

4. Sure   Not Sure   8. Sure   Not Sure

C. Practice.   Now practice intonation with tag questions. Ask the questions that you just heard in Exercise B. Follow the cues at the beginning of each question: Sure = Use falling intonation; Not sure = Use rising intonation.

1. (Not sure) Chrissy's smart, isn't she?

2. (Not sure) Evan has a great job this summer, doesn't he?

3. (Sure) You always land on your feet, don't you, Brandon?

4. (Sure) Chrissy's smart, isn't she?

5. (Sure) That video game is doing well, isn't it?

6. (Not sure) Using programmers in Eastern Europe isn't fair to American workers, is it?

7. (Not sure) You're not leaving now, are you?

8. (Sure) You worked in a video store last summer, didn't you, Brandon?

Pronunciation

Reduced Forms of Words in Tag Questions (Audio)

In natural conversation, some words (and combinations of sounds) become reduced, or shortened. Here are some examples:

Long Form	Short Form
You got a good job, <u>didn't you</u>?	You got a good job, <u>didncha</u>?
You didn't know that, <u>did you</u>?	You didn't know that, <u>didja</u>?
You always have good luck, <u>don't you</u>?	You always have good luck, <u>doncha</u>?
You're taking Econ 1, <u>aren't you</u>?	You're taking Econ 1, <u>arncha</u>?

D. Practice. (Audio) Listen to the questions. You'll hear the reduced forms. Fill in the blanks with the long forms.

1. You got a great summer job, _____?
2. You didn't study last night, _____?
3. You're pretty lucky, _____?
4. You think you're pretty smart, _____?
5. You're working for a computer company, _____?
6. You didn't get an internship this summer, _____?

Review: Language Functions

Asking for Confirmation and Offering an Explanation (Video/Audio)

Listen again to these examples of asking for confirmation and offering an explanation. Pay attention to the intonation of tag questions and the reductions. If you watch the video, also pay attention to facial expressions. You'll use these functions in the next section.

Put It Together

A. Making Assumptions.   Your teacher will select a partner for you to talk to. Before you work with your partner, think of some assumptions about this person. Use the following list of personal qualities and conditions, or make up your own assumptions. Make some assumptions that you are sure about and others that you are not so sure about. Take notes on your assumptions.

Personal Qualities and Conditions		
smart	good summer job	bad summer job
good student	bad student	lucky
unlucky	rich	studies a lot
doesn't study a lot	likes his/her teachers	doesn't like his/her teachers
your ideas: _____		

B. Making Assumptions and Offering Explanations. **Pair**   Now tell your partner your assumptions. Practice using both kinds of tag question intonation: falling if you're sure, and rising if you're not sure. Your partner can answer any way: agreeing, disagreeing, correcting you, or giving more information. Then exchange roles.

. . : : : : **Part Four** Broadcast English: Transitional Economy in Mongolia

Before Listening

A. Thinking Ahead. **Group**   You're going to listen to part of a radio program about the economy of Mongolia. In order to prepare for the program, discuss the answers to these questions.

• Based on what you know about Mongolia from Part One of this chapter, what positive changes are occurring there? What negative changes?

Mongolia

The Mongolian
Stock Exchange
in the capital city
of Ulan Batur

A horse race on the steppes outside Ulan Batur

B. Vocabulary Preparation.   In the radio program, you are going to hear some words that may be new to you. Before you listen, guess the meaning of some of the words from the radio program. The words are underlined in the sentences. Look for clues to their meaning in the words around them.

   Write your guess in the blank after each sentence. Compare your answers with a partner's. Then check your guess with your teacher or the dictionary.

1. This antique map is very valuable: It shows every place in <u>the known world</u> in the year 1400.

   Guess: _____

2. In the 1980s, he lived in a government <u>collective</u> in Mongolia. There, everyone worked and lived cooperatively in one place. Now he owns his own farm and he works for himself.

   Guess: _____

3. The example I saw was <u>eye-popping</u>; I was so surprised, I could hardly believe what I saw.

   Guess: _____

4. Poverty is <u>widespread</u> in Mongolia; many people all over the country are having a difficult time finding work and enough food to eat.

   Guess: _____

5. Jocelyn wanted to meet Mr. Bolt in his office, but he wasn't there. She finally <u>caught up with</u> him at a horse race so she interviewed him there.

   Guess: _____

6. Western politicians always shake hands with voters; <u>pumping the flesh</u> is something they do at every opportunity.

   Guess: _____

7. Even though she's famous, she's very <u>down to earth</u>. I feel comfortable talking to her because she's just like ordinary people.

   Guess: _____

8. The bookstore's supply of notebooks is <u>dwindling</u>; there are only two left.

   Guess: _____

9. His economic philosophy is very clear: He believes in the <u>gospel</u> of "The rising tide lifts all boats."

   Guess: _____

10. Her work as a business reporter takes her to the <u>far-flung</u> corners of the earth. Just last week she was interviewing a politician in Mongolia.

   Guess: _____

C. Vocabulary: Stock Market Terms.

In the radio program, you are going to hear some stock market terms. First, read each sentence and guess the meaning of the underlined words. Then choose their meaning from the definitions in the box. Write the letters in the blanks.

The New York
Stock Exchange

Sentences

_____ 1. We visited the <u>stock exchange</u> when we went to New York. It was very exciting: People were running around, shouting, and tossing papers everywhere as they bought and sold stocks.

_____ 2. Most high-tech stocks in the United States are listed on the <u>NASDAQ</u> exchange.

_____ 3. BioData <u>shareholders</u> were upset when they learned that the company lost money last year. Later, they voted to fire the company's president.

_____ 4. I don't want to buy stock through that <u>brokerage</u> company because it charges too much in fees.

_____ 5. <u>Volume</u> is very small at the Mongolian stock exchange. There isn't a great deal of buying and selling because there aren't a lot of businesses yet.

_____ 6. In Mongolia people are now <u>trading</u> stocks using computers, but using high technology to buy and sell stocks has been common in many parts of the world for several years.

_____ 7. Minisoft Corporation is selling its stock for $10 a <u>share</u>. I had an extra $1,000, so I bought 100 shares.

Definitions

a. the amount of shares that are bought or sold

b. a part into which the ownership of a company is divided

c. one of the stock exchanges in the United States (the National Association of Securities Dealers Automated Quotations)

d. the place where stocks are bought and sold

e. people who own shares of stock in a company

f. a company whose business it is to buy and sell stock for its customers

g. buying and selling

Listening

A. Listening for the Main Idea. <Audio> The radio passage for this chapter is part of a program called *Marketplace*. In it, Jocelyn Ford reports on conditions in Mongolia since it became a market economy. As you listen to the radio program the first time, try to answer this question:

- What are some examples of change in Mongolia?

B. Listening for Details. <Audio> Listen again to part of the program. Listen for the answer to the following question and write your answer in the blanks.

- What word would you use to describe Mongolia's stock market? Give examples to support your choice.

  The Mongolian stock market is _____

  Examples: _____

  _____

C. Listening for Reasons. <Audio> Listen again to short parts of the program. Write your answers to the following questions; write just phrases, not complete sentences. You'll hear each part two times.

1. Why have so many Mongolians invested in the stock market?

   _____

   _____

2. Why did Mr. Bolt go to the horse race?

   _____

   _____

3. Why isn't there enough fermented mare's milk in UB (Ulan Batur)?

   _____

   _____

listening Strategy

Listening for Indirect Causes [Audio]

Speakers sometimes explain a reason or cause for something using a chain of causes. This is because sometimes one condition leads to another, which in turn leads to another. Here is an example:

A causes B and B causes C

As a result of increased computer use, American children spend more time indoors. The effect of this has been that American children are less physically fit than ever before.

In this sentence, A represents increased computer use. Increased computer use causes B, the fact that children spend more time indoors. Fact B in turn causes C, the fact that children are less physically fit.

Another structure can express a causal chain:

C is the result of B, which is the result of A

American children are less physically fit than ever. This is due to the fact that they spend much more time indoors as a result of increased computer use.

In this sentence, C (children are less physically fit) is the result of B (increased time indoors), which in turn is the result of A (increased computer use).

Speakers express indirect causes using the same kind of language that you hear in simple cause and result statements:

Emphasizing Causes	**Emphasizing Results**
X causes Y	X is a result of Y
a cause of X is Y	a result of X is Y

Other words for expressing causes and results are

- effect (One <u>effect</u> of increased computer use is that kids today are less physically fit.)
- influence (TV has a negative <u>influence</u> on children's behavior.)
- impact (Increased computer use has had an <u>impact</u> on physical fitness.)
- make (Too much TV <u>makes</u> kids fat.)

D. Listening for an Indirect Cause. [Audio]   Listen to another part of the program. Listen for the following information:

Explain how Mongolia's connection to the Internet has led to an increase in tourism. Write your explanation in the blanks.

_____

_____

_____

listening Strategy

Listening to Numerical Information (Audio)

You often hear numerical information when you listen to speakers discussing economics. Numerical information includes the following:

numbers of people or things: 100,000 inhabitants

amounts of money: 50 million dollars

fractions: a quarter of the population

percents: a 50 percent reduction

E. Listening for Numerical Information. (Audio)   Listen again to parts of the program. This time, listen for numerical information. Complete each passage with the numerical information that you hear.

1. It's now the Mongolian stock exchange. Volume is tiny, about _____ dollars a day, but according to a spokeswoman for the exchange, it's as high-tech an operation as anywhere in the world.

2. _____ of Mongolia's population is—an amazing _____ people—are shareholders.

3. A _____ of the population lives below the poverty line, inflation is over _____ percent, and unemployment is widespread.

4. This spring, Mongolia got its first satellite connection to the Internet. The technology has helped reduce communication costs to the outside world from _____ dollars a minute, to a mere _____ cents.

After Listening

A. Discussion. **Group**   Discuss the answers to these questions.

1. Would you like to visit Mongolia as a tourist? Why or why not?

2. Make predictions about Mongolia's future, based on what you have heard and read in this chapter. Think about the following:

   • further results of being connected to the Internet

   • results of increased tourism

   • how modernization may affect the traditional way of life in Mongolia

B. (Optional) Applying Your Knowledge.   If you have a VCR and access to a video rental store, rent the movie *The Herders of the Mongun-Taiga* (1989), about the culture of the Tuvans, a nomadic herding tribe in Mongolia. Notice in it the examples of the traditional ways of life that may be disappearing in Mongolia. Report your findings to the class.

. : : : : : **Part Five** Academic English: Emerging Nations
                              in a Global Economy

Before Listening

listening Strategy

Reviewing What You Already Know/Realizing What You Don't Know

As you saw in Chapter One, lectures sometimes build on information that you have already studied. Other times, they present information that is entirely new to you. You usually know the topic of a lecture, however, because it is indicated in your syllabus or because it is related to material in your textbook. When you know the topic of a lecture, it's a good idea to think about what you already know about the subject, and to realize what you *don't* know about it. This prepares you for the information that you will hear and helps you focus your attention while you listen.

A. Brainstorming: Reviewing What You Already Know. Group   The lecture that you are going to hear discusses the differences between two economic systems: socialism and market capitalism. Before you listen, fill in the following chart with all of the information about the two systems that you and your group members can think of. Use this list to help you review what you already know.

- examples of countries that have or had each type of economy
- the role of the government in each type of economy
- the pros and cons of each type of economy

	Socialism	**Market Capitalism**
Countries		
Role of Government		
Pros/Cons		
Other		

B. Thinking Ahead: Realizing What You Don't Know

1. Look over the picture and the partial outline on pages 187–191 for the lecture. What questions do you expect (or want) the speaker to answer? Is there anything that you're curious about? Write your questions in the blanks.

_____

_____

_____

_____

2. Now look over the questions in the Comprehension Check on pages 192–193. Are any of these similar to your own questions?

C. Guessing Meaning from Context.

In the lecture, you are going to hear some words that may be new to you. Before you listen, guess the meaning of some of the words from the lecture. The words are underlined in the sentences. Look for clues to their meaning in the words around them.

Write your guess in the blank after each sentence. Then check your guess with your teacher or the dictionary.

1. The garden is large, but right now it's <u>sparsely</u> planted. There's a lot of empty space left for the fruit trees next summer.

   Guess: _____

2. Paying taxes is <u>inherent in</u> being a citizen; you can't avoid it.

   Guess: _____

3. We were impressed by the <u>magnitude</u> of her generosity. She gave the school well over one million dollars.

   Guess: _____

4. I felt <u>constrained</u> by the strict rules at my high school, so I asked my parents to send me to one where there was more freedom.

   Guess: _____

5. The student gave a <u>plausible</u> excuse for why he was absent, so the teacher let him take a make-up exam.

   Guess: _____

6. My new boss drives me crazy because he <u>micromanages</u> everything; he wants to control every detail of every project I work on.

   Guess: _____

7. Maribel has no friends; she spends such an <u>inordinate</u> amount of time studying that she has no time left for social activities.

   Guess: _____

8. Only the <u>elite</u> in Xenrovia—the wealthy and people who worked for the government—had access to foreign luxury products.

   Guess: _____

9. Their relationship requires a lot of <u>give and take</u>. For example, Max drives Sam to work, but Sam buys the gas.

Guess: _____

10. Mongolia has an <u>emerging</u> economy: It used to be socialist, and now it is developing a market economy.

Guess: _____

Listening

A. Vocabulary: Economics Terms. **Audio**   Listen to the following economics words and terms in context. Each one has a meaning in the list on the right. Write the letter of the meaning next to the word it matches.

Words/Terms   **Definitions**

_____ **1.** a trade-off   *a.* economic planners in socialist government

_____ **2.** centralize   *b.* the exchange of one thing for another

_____ **3.** decentralized   *c.* to put power or authority in a central organization

_____ **4.** technocrats   *d.* to give power or authority to private citizens

_____ **5.** the private sector   *e.* handling money in a smart way

_____ **6.** strategic output   *f.* not the government; private citizens

_____ **7.** fiscally sound   *g.* a lack or a small amount of something

_____ **8.** scarcity   *h.* materials or products that help a country defend itself

_____ **9.** abundance   *i.* a great quantity

_____ **10.** privatize   *j.* power distributed among several groups

B. Listening for the Main Idea. **Audio**   You'll hear a lecture titled "Emerging Nations in a Global Economy." Listen once to the entire lecture. (You'll listen again later.) As you listen this time, don't take notes. Instead, follow along with the outline and keep this question in mind.

• According to the lecture, what are some of the main differences between socialism and market capitalism?

Emerging Nations in a Global Economy

I. Introduction: What Are the Main Points of the Lecture?

   A. Economics issues that affect ___all nations of the world_____

   B. _____ ways nations have chosen to deal with them

   C. The disadvantages of one system that have led to major trend in economics in the

      last decade: _____

II. Economics Issues That Affect All Nations of the World

   A. Number of nations: _____

   B. Ways in which nations differ:

      1. Range in age + examples: _____

         _____

      2. Size vs. population + examples: _____

         _____

      3. Wealth, measured in resources. Examples:

         a. Human, such as _____

            _____

         b. Natural, such as _____

            _____

         c. Some nations may be rich in human resources and poor in natural, such as

            _____

   C. Even though nations differ, they fit together to form the _____

      _____

   D. All nations are constrained by the scarcity of _____

      _____

      1. Scarcity affects all nations because _____

         _____

      2. Nothing is free; everything _____

E. "Cost" means _____

   1. "There is no free lunch" means _____

      _____

      a. Example: _____

         _____

      b. Explanation of example: ("Economists say") _____

         _____

      c. General example: _____

         _____

   2. A "trade-off" is _____

      _____

III. How Nations Deal With Trade-Offs: Two Ways

   A. #1: Definition/explanation of socialism: _____

      _____

      _____

   B. #2: Definition/explanation of market capitalism: _____

      _____

      _____

IV. Under Socialism

   A. Who did economic planning? _____

   B. These people were responsible for plans for

      1. How _____

      2. What _____

      3. For whom _____

   C. The plans were plausible because _____

      _____

   D. The central plan was not simple because

      1. _____ and

      2. _____

   E. Technocrats' priorities

      1. Used resources to produce _____

      _____

      2. Gave priority to "strategic output": _____

      _____

      3. Consumers had to _____

      _____

   F. Planners used power of the state to _____

      _____

      1. Example in the 1960s: _____

      _____

      2. "Bury" meant _____

      _____

      3. Therefore, to achieve these objectives, Soviets had to _____

      _____

      _____

V. Economic Results of Socialism

   A. No unemployment; for example _____; however,

      _____

B. Emphasis on strategic production

    1. Result: _____

    2. Technocrats determined that _____

        _____

    3. Emphasis on strategic production led to _____ because

        _____

    4. Examples of shortages:

        a. _____

            _____

            _____

        b. _____

            _____

            _____

    5. Shortages not only posed _____

        _____

        but also _____

        _____

C. Wages

    1. Dependable but little to _____

    2. Only choice for saving: _____

    3. Banks used savings for loans for _____

    4. But loans were essentially _____

        that enabled strategic industries to _____

        _____

    5. Government bank supplemented loans and credits by _____

        _____

    6. Printing money resulted in _____ ;

        as a result, consumers had to _____

        _____

    D. Central planning also resulted in _____,

_____, and _____.

    E. All these conditions resulted in _____

_____

      1. Socialism was a _____

      2. Central planning managed to _____

VI. The Transition to Market Capitalism

    A. Market capitalism substitutes _____

_____ for

_____

    B. But path slow and difficult

      1. One costly result: _____

_____

      2. Other results include _____

_____

C. Taking Notes. [Audio]   Listen to the entire lecture again. This time fill in the outline.

D. Using Your Notes.   Answer as many of these questions as you can, either from memory or from your notes. Don't worry yet about the ones you can't answer. You'll have another chance to listen. Work alone.

1. How do we measure the wealth of a nation? _____

_____

2. What economic reality must all nations face? _____

_____

3. What is the "cost" of producing the things that people need? _____

_____

4. What are some examples of "give and take" or "quid pro quo"? _____

_____

5. In which two main ways have nations tried to deal with trade-offs? _____

_____

6. How are socialism and capitalism different? _____

_____

_____

7. Who made economic decisions in a socialist economy? What usually were the priorities in

socialism economies? _____

_____

_____

8. What difficulties do countries face as they make the transition from socialism to market

capitalism? _____

_____

_____

E. Listening for Specific Information. **Audio**   Listen again to the entire lecture. This time listen specifically for the answers to any questions that you left blank in Exercise D.

F. (Optional) Filling in the Gaps. **Audio**   If necessary, listen one last time to the entire lecture and fill in any gaps in your outline.

After Listening

A. Comprehension Check. **Pair**   Use your notes to write your answers to these questions. When you finish, compare your answers with a partner's.

1. How does the lecturer define socialism? _____

_____

2. How does the lecturer define market capitalism? _____

_____

3. What are some characteristics of socialism? _____

_____

4. What were some of the positive results of socialism? What were some of the negative results?

_____

_____

5. Why have many countries turned from socialism to market capitalism? _____

_____

B. Discussion. **Group**   The lecture presented a lot of information about socialism and little about market capitalism. In particular, it gave a lot of detail on the failures of socialist systems, but it didn't give the same kinds of details on market capitalism. In your group, discuss the answer to these questions.

1. What are the benefits of market capitalism, in your opinion?

2. What are some of the negative aspects of market capitalism?

Step Beyond

A. Choosing a Topic.   Choose *one* of the projects on page 194 to do either by yourself or in a small group.

academic Strategy

Choosing a Topic

Occasionally you will have a choice of topics or assignments in a class that you are taking. You often don't have much time to make a choice, and you certainly don't have time to make a choice and then change your mind. Therefore, it's a good idea to have some strategies for making good, quick topic choices. Here are some things to think about when you choose a topic. You should be able to answer "yes" to at least two of these when you choose a topic:

- Are you curious about or interested in the topic?
- Do you already know something about it?
- Even if you don't know much about it, do you have a pretty good idea of how or where to get information on it?
- Do you have enough time to get all the necessary information and do a good job on it?

Practice.   Look at the following list of topics. Read them quickly. Which could you talk about for 3–5 minutes if you had one night to prepare? Put a check (✓) next to good choices for you.

_____ **1.** how the stock market works

_____ **2.** the differences between socialism and market capitalism

_____ **3.** the history of Mongolia

_____ **4.** a few facts about recent changes in Mongolia

_____ **5.** using the Web to do research

_____ **6.** how to use a PC

_____ **7.** my career goals

_____ **8.** the best way to learn a foreign language

Project 1

Find another transitional economy (such as Mongolia) that is changing because of the effects of technology and/or tourism. Do Web or library research on the country. Find out as much as you can about the traditional culture of the country. Then find facts about the increase of technology and/or tourism in the country. Finally, find specific examples of how technology and/or tourism have affected the traditional way of life in the country you chose.

Project 2

Do Web or library research to find an example of a country that is experiencing a difficult transition from socialism to market capitalism. Find examples that support the main points of the lecture that you heard. Look for the following information:

• What was the country like when it had a socialist economy? What were the conditions? What was good about the economy and conditions? What was bad?

• Why did the country change to market capitalism? When did this transition start?

• What problems is the country currently facing? What are people doing to correct the problems?

speaking Strategy

Giving a Report from Notes

When you give a report, it's a good idea to speak from notes, not to read complete sentences that you have written. One way to do this is to make an outline of what you want to discuss. Read your outline many times—try to memorize it. Then make a less detailed outline, with just the main points (for example, the Roman numeral heads and the capital letter heads). See if you can remember the missing details. Then make an outline with only the Roman heads. When you can give your report by just glancing at these heads, you're ready to speak in front of the class. This way, you can make eye contact and be a more interesting speaker.

B. Reporting Your Information.   Organize your notes. Then give a brief report (3–5 minutes) to the class on what you have learned. Think about including pictures, charts, or any other visual material that is relevant to your topic. When you give your report, make sure you just glance at your notes—don't read them. Finally, listen carefully to your classmates' reports. Try to think of a question to ask the speaker to show that you are paying attention.

unit 4

Ecology

chapter Seven

Endangered Species

In this chapter, you'll read about one endangered species, tigers. You'll also listen to information about and discuss other endangered plants and animals and efforts to save them.

`. : : : :` **Part One** Introduction: A Future for Tigers?

A. Thinking Ahead. `Pair`   Look at the photos of some endangered species and answer these questions.

1. In what parts of the world or habitats do the species in the photos live?

2. What are some other endangered species? What are their habitats?

3. Why are these and other species facing extinction?

4. What are some measures that people have taken to help correct the problem of endangered species? Do you know of any species* that used to be endangered but is off the endangered species list?

5. What do you know about tigers? In what parts of the world do they live? What threatens their survival?

Endangered Species

Northeastern
beach tiger beetle

Hooded crane

Bobcat

*Note: The word *species* is both singular and plural.

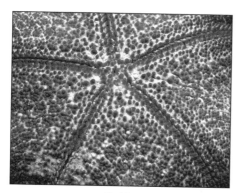

Urchin

Nile crocodile

Pahrump killifish

Slow loris

Indigo macaw

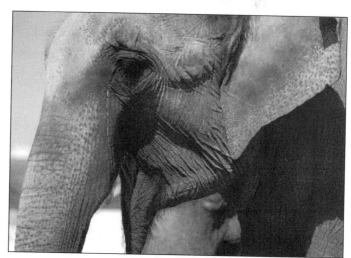

Asian elephant

B. Reading.   The following article about tigers is by Peter Jackson, the chairman of the Cat Specialist Group at the World Conservation Union (IUCN) in Switzerland. As you read, try to answer this question:

• *Is* there a future for tigers?

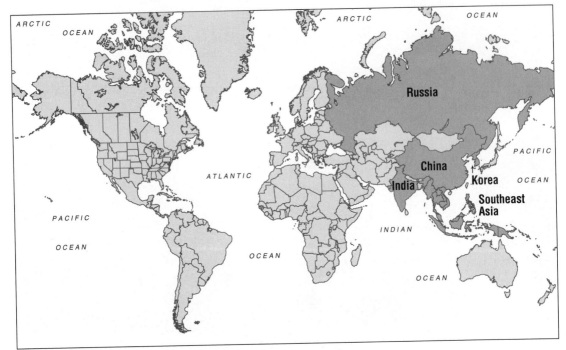

The countries where tigers live

A Future for Tigers?

Humans and tigers have lived together since time immemorial at the top of food chains that form part of the complex web of life on earth. They have lived their lives aware of, but not dependent on, each other's existence. Today, humans dominate the world, and the tiger is at their mercy.

Throughout the ages, the tiger has had a remarkable impact on the human mind. Millions of Hindus worship the image of Durga, the powerful

Bengal tiger

female deity, who rides a tiger. Siva, the Hindu God of Destruction and Creation, is enthroned on a tiger skin. Tigers appear in Buddhist culture in China, Korea, and Japan. In the forests, tribal people still tend simple shrines to the tiger. And many Asians believe that tiger bones can cure diseases. In the western world, the tiger has inspired art and

15 poetry, and has been adopted as the advertising symbol of leading businesses. Yet we humans are close to wiping out this majestic animal.

Nobody really knows how many wild tigers there are. Counting such a secretive animal is immensely difficult, and most estimates are simply guesses. However, there may be between 5,000 and 7,500—a small fraction of the 100,000 that may have roamed the

20 forests a century ago. The tiger's present plight is due to an exploding human population, which has converted wild lands for settlement and agriculture, ruthlessly hunted not only the tiger's prey, but the tiger itself. Three of the eight subspecies—Bali, Javan, and Caspian—are already extinct, and the South China tiger is near extinction. Can the others survive the coming century?

Siberian tiger

25 Most people associate tigers with hot climates, but in Russia, China, and Korea tigers thrive in winter snows and sub-zero temperatures. They are widely known as Siberian tigers, but, in fact, their home is not the dark coniferous forests that stretch across northern Russia; they live in deciduous forests in latitudes similar to those between Rome and Berlin. They are best referred to as Amur tigers, from the Amur river basin, which has

30 always been their homeland.

The collapse of Soviet Russia created a crisis for the Amur tiger. As the economy became disorganized, law and order collapsed. People in the Russian Far East, traditionally hunters, began to compete with tigers for deer and wild boar as food. They hunted the

tiger itself for its bones and other body parts, which were in demand in China for medicine;
35 and its skins, which they could sell for as much as $10,000 in Japan and South Korea.
Poaching reached serious levels between 1992 and 1994. At one point, the tiger population appeared to have been reduced to fewer than 200. International organizations sent
money to help anti-poaching teams, which lessened the problem somewhat. In addition,
a ban in China strengthened border controls on the illegal trade in tiger products.

40   Meanwhile, Russian and American scientists observed tigers and analyzed their footprints in order to estimate their numbers in the winter of 1995 to 1996. The results were
heartening: 330–371 adults and 85–94 cubs. Clearly the Amur tiger was surviving.

On the other hand, India is the home to more than half the world's surviving 5,000–
7,500 tigers, but the population has been heavily disturbed by loss of habitat. Only three
45 reserves are estimated to have over 100 tigers, and some have fewer than 30.

Does the wild tiger have a future? Because they live in isolated small groups, they are
threatened by poaching and genetic deterioration through inbreeding. These factors, along
with continued habitat loss due to human use, suggest that their numbers will continue
to decline. The larger sub-populations (such as the Amur) have a reasonable chance. But
50 ultimately, the tiger will live on only if humans allow it to.

The extinction of the wild tiger—a powerful symbol of the natural world—would
provoke a deep sense of loss among many people. Not only would it remove a key species
from the web of life on which we all depend, but it would bode ill for the survival of other
threatened wildlife, perhaps even for ourselves if the natural foundations of life continue
55 to be destroyed.

Source: Peter Jackson, adapted and excerpted from "A Future for Tigers?" from *People & the Planet* 7, no. 4, (1998). Copyright © 1998 by People and the Planet. Reprinted with the permission of the publishers.

C. Vocabulary Check.   Find words or expressions in the reading passage that mean the following:

1. existing since before we can remember = _____

2. under their power = _____

3. a supreme being; a god or goddess = _____

4. sitting on a throne, like a king = _____

5. bad situation or conditions = _____

6. stealing animals = _____

7. a law forbidding something = _____

8. encouraging = _____

9. be a bad sign = _____

D. Discussion. Group Discuss the answers to these questions.

1. Does the tiger have any special meaning to you or to your culture?

2. How must humans change in order to preserve endangered species such as the tiger? Are most human groups willing and/or able to make these changes? Explain your answer.

3. What does Jackson mean when he says: "Not only would it remove a key species from the web of life on which we all depend, but it would bode ill for the survival of other threatened wildlife, perhaps even for ourselves if the natural foundations of life continue to be destroyed"?

E. Freewriting. Choose *one* of these topics. Write about it for fifteen minutes. Don't worry about grammar and don't use a dictionary. Just put as many ideas as you can on paper.

• your reaction to the reading

• what tigers mean to you or to someone from your culture

• an endangered species that you know about and/or the efforts to preserve it

∴ ⋮ ⋮ **Part Two** Everyday English: Counting Jaguars

Before Listening

A. Thinking Ahead. Group You are going to hear Evan, Victor, and Chrissy talk about a possible way to spend summer vacation. Before you listen, discuss the answers to these questions.

1. What are some reasons for doing a volunteer job during the summer (or other breaks in the school year)?

2. What are some possible volunteer jobs that might help preserve endangered species? Where might these jobs be?

3. Students in certain majors might be particularly interested in volunteering for an organization that helps preserve endangered species. What majors might these be?

4. Have you ever joined or done any work for an organization that preserves wildlife or worked in some way to protect the environment? If so, share your experiences with your group members.

B. Vocabulary Preparation: Informal Expressions.   The students in the conversation that you'll hear use some words and informal expressions that are commonly found in casual conversation. First, read each sentence and guess the meaning of the underlined words. Then choose their meaning from the definitions in the box. Write the letters in the blanks.

Definitions

a. a unique opportunity   *e.* a hidden difficulty or cost

b. to say it simply   *f.* we were just talking about you/him/her

c. can't participate   *g.* yes

d. wait

Sentences

_____   **1.** You want me to write that down? Okay, but <u>hold on</u>—I have to find a pen first.

_____   **2.** Do I want a fun summer job? <u>Yep</u>, of course I do!

_____   **3.** <u>Speak of the devil</u> . . . he just walked in. I'll put him on the phone.

_____   **4.** He's smart, he's got a lot of money, he's handsome. . . <u>in one word</u>—perfect!

_____   **5.** There's got to be <u>a catch</u>. You don't get something for nothing.

_____   **6.** Well, <u>I'm out</u>. I can't afford that kind of trip. You guys go ahead without me.

_____   **7.** This is <u>the chance of a lifetime</u>. You'll probably never again have an opportunity to see tigers in their natural habitat.

Listening

A. Listening for the Main Idea. (Video/Audio) You're going to hear the students talk about Victor's ideas for a summer job. Listen to the entire conversation. As you listen, try to answer this question:

- What is "the catch" to Victor's idea?

B. Listening for Details. (Video/Audio) Listen again to the conversation. Then write your answers to these questions. Write short phrases, not complete sentences.

1. For whom is Evan taking a message?

_____

2. What animals can you study in Hawaii, according to Victor?

_____

3. What kind of research does the organization sponsor?

_____

4. What can you do in the Mexican forest?

_____

5. What can you do in Costa Rica?

_____

6. Do you have to be an expert to work for the organization?

_____

7. How much does it cost to count jaguars?

_____

C. Listening for Inferences. Video/Audio   Listen again to short parts of the conversation. What can you infer from each? Circle the letter of the best answer.

1. How does Victor feel about his idea for the summer?

   a. bored

   b. excited

   c. worried

2. When Chrissy hears Victor say "exotic locations," how does she react?

   a. She becomes very interested.

   b. She feels disappointed.

   c. She doesn't believe Victor.

3. How does Evan interpret the word "volunteer"?

   a. It sounds like fun.

   b. It sounds like school.

   c. It sounds like work.

4. What does Chrissy think when Victor says that you don't have to be an expert?

   a. She believes him.

   b. She doesn't understand him.

   c. She doesn't quite believe him.

5. What is Evan doing when he says that Victor is on his way to count jaguars?

   a. He's telling the truth.

   b. He's making a joke.

   c. He's lying.

After Listening

A. Information Gap: Where in the World? **Pair**   Work with a partner. Find out about current endangered species: their names, habitats, and reasons for endangerment. One partner will work on page 210 and the other on page 265. Don't look at your partner's page. Take turns asking and answering questions about endangered species. Write your answers in the boxes on the chart. Ask your partner questions such as these:

• Where does the panda live?

• Why is the panda endangered?

• What endangered species lives in China?

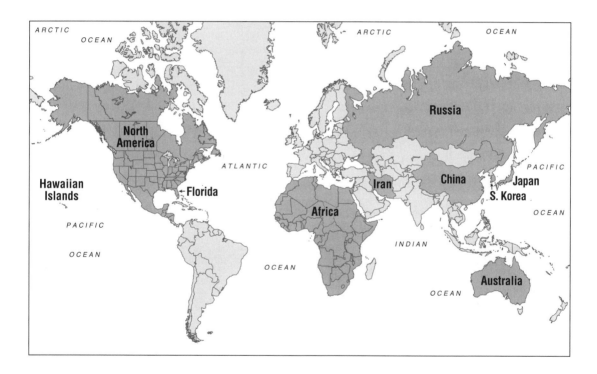

Student A

Endangered Species: Where in the World?

Endangered Species	Habitat	Reasons for Endangerment
	China	• China's warming climate • Loss of habitat
Cheetah		• Loss of habitat • Inbreeding (and thus genetic anomalies) • Poaching
Uhiuhi tree	Hawaiian Islands	
Queensland koala	Australia	
Blue karner butterfly		• Loss of habitat due to development
Oriental white stork	Russia, China, South Korea, and Japan	
European tree frog	Northwest Africa, the whole of Eurasia (with the exception of Great Britain), and the Japanese archipelago	
Short horned lizard		• Agricultural expansion • Oil and gas exploration
Florida manatee	Coastal waters of Florida and Georgia	
	All oceans of the world	• Hunting

Source: Table: "Endangered Species: Where in the World?" adapted from a website produced by the IWC Volunteer Webweaver Team. Available from http://iwc.org/volunteers/archives/May98/; INTERNET. Copyright © 1998 by the International Wildlife Coalition. Reprinted with permission.

B. Discussion. (Group) Discuss the answers to these questions.

1. Were you surprised by any of the information that you learned from this activity? What surprised you? Why?

2. What endangered species are native to the region that you were born in? To the region that you live in now?

. : : : : Part Three The Mechanics of Listening and Speaking

Language Functions

Answering the Phone (Audio)

You can answer your home phone simply by saying "Hello." (Businesspeople usually answer with their full name—e.g., "Evan Connor"—or the name of the business.) If the caller asks to speak with you, here is what you can say:

- Speaking.
- This is Evan.
- This is he/she.

Finding Out Who's Calling (Audio)

If the caller asks to speak with another person who is there, it's often a good idea to find out who is calling before you pass the phone to him or her. Here are some ways to do this:

- May I ask who's calling?
- Can I tell him who's calling?
- May I tell her who's calling?

Taking a Phone Message (Audio)

If the caller asks to speak with another person who isn't there, here is what you can say:

- He's not here right now. Would you like me to give him a message?
- She just stepped out. May I take a message?
- He isn't available right now. May I give him a message?

A. Practice. (Audio)   Listen to these phone calls and fill in the information on the message notes.

1.
Telephone Message

To _____
Here is a Message for You

From _____

Phone No. _____ Ext. _____

☐ Telephoned ☐ Will Call Again
☐ Returned Your Call ☐ Came to See You
☐ Please Phone ☐ Wants to See You

Taken by _____

Date _____ Time _____

2.
Telephone Message

To _____
Here is a Message for You

From _____

Phone No. _____ Ext. _____

☐ Telephoned ☐ Will Call Again
☐ Returned Your Call ☐ Came to See You
☐ Please Phone ☐ Wants to See You

Taken by _____

Date _____ Time _____

3.
Telephone Message

To _____
Here is a Message for You

From _____

Phone No. _____ Ext. _____

☐ Telephoned ☐ Will Call Again
☐ Returned Your Call ☐ Came to See You
☐ Please Phone ☐ Wants to See You

Taken by _____

Date _____ Time _____

4.
Telephone Message

To _____
Here is a Message for You

From _____

Phone No. _____ Ext. _____

☐ Telephoned ☐ Will Call Again
☐ Returned Your Call ☐ Came to See You
☐ Please Phone ☐ Wants to See You

Taken by _____

Date _____ Time _____

Language Function

Asking for Clarification/Clarifying `Audio`

When you take a message over the phone, you don't always hear clearly, so it's important to be able to ask for clarification. Here are several ways to do that:

- Excuse me?
- What was that again?
- Could you please repeat that?

- Can you say that again, please?
- How do you spell that?

Because some letters sound the same as others over the phone, it helps also to give a common word or name beginning with that letter. Here are some examples:

B as in *boy*	*S* as in *Sam*
D as in *dog*	*T* as in *Tom*
F as in *Frank*	*V* as in *Victor*
P as in *Paul*	*Z* as in *zebra*

B. Practice. `Audio`   Listen to these parts of conversations in which one person asks for clarification and another clarifies information. Fill in the message notes here and on the next page.

1.

Telephone Message

To _____
Here is a Message for You

From _____

Phone No. _____ Ext. _____

☐ Telephoned   ☐ Will Call Again
☐ Returned Your Call   ☐ Came to See You
☐ Please Phone   ☐ Wants to See You

Taken by _____

Date _____ Time _____

2.

Telephone Message

To _____
Here is a Message for You

From _____

Phone No. _____ Ext. _____

☐ Telephoned   ☐ Will Call Again
☐ Returned Your Call   ☐ Came to See You
☐ Please Phone   ☐ Wants to See You

Taken by _____

Date _____ Time _____

3.

Telephone Message

To _____

Here is a Message for You

| |
| |
| |
| |

From _____

Phone No. _____ Ext. _____

☐ Telephoned   ☐ Will Call Again
☐ Returned Your Call   ☐ Came to See You
☐ Please Phone   ☐ Wants to See You

Taken by_____

Date _____ Time _____

4.

Telephone Message

To _____

Here is a Message for You

| |
| |
| |
| |

From _____

Phone No. _____ Ext. _____

☐ Telephoned   ☐ Will Call Again
☐ Returned Your Call   ☐ Came to See You
☐ Please Phone   ☐ Wants to See You

Taken by_____

Date _____ Time _____

Pronunciation

Can and *Can't* Audio

In some cases, the words *can* and *can't* might sound the same to you because you don't always hear the *-t* in *can't*. This is especially true when a word beginning with *-t* or *-d* follows these words. Three suggestions follow:

1. Use the context to help you understand. Here is an example:

    "I'm sorry, but I can't talk right now."

2. You can ask for clarification. Here is an example:

    Did you say *can* or *can't?*

3. Listen for stress and the vowel sound: Is it the full /æ/ sound in *can't* or the reduced /ə/ sound in *can?* Don't worry about the *-t* at the end.

C. Practice. **Audio**   Listen to the pronunciation of *can* and *can't* in these sentences. Repeat each statement after the speaker.

1. *a.* I can help you.

    b. I can't help you.

2. *a.* She can drive.

    b. She can't drive.

3. *a.* He can do it later.

    b. He can't do it later.

4. *a.* He can take a message.

    b. He can't take a message.

5. *a.* You can leave a message.

    b. You can't leave a message.

6. *a.* We can tell him tomorrow.

    b. We can't tell him tomorrow.

D. Practice. **Audio**   Listen to each sentence. Does the speaker say *can* or *can't?* Write the word that you hear.

1. _____

2. _____

3. _____

4. _____

5. _____

6. _____

7. _____

8. _____

9. _____

10. _____

11. _____

12. _____

Language Function

Recording an Outgoing Message   **Audio**

If you have an answering machine, you'll need to record an outgoing message, of course. This should be short, concise, and clear. You might leave your full name, your first name, and/or your phone number. Depending on who is likely to call you, and the reasons for their calls, your message can be informal or formal. If you use your phone only for personal calls, an informal message is adequate. If you use your phone for business, or to speak to professors or employers, you might want a more formal message. Here are some examples:

Hi. This is Jason. I can't come to the phone right now, so leave a message. (Informal)

Hello. You have reached 924-555-1234. Please leave a message, and we'll get back to you as soon as we can. (Formal)

Notice that the second example doesn't indicate a person's name (only the number) and that the subject of the sentence is "we." This is a good choice for people who might not want callers to know their name or that they live alone.

Note: When you *leave* a message, leave your name and/or phone number and the time you called. It's usually best to leave a brief, concise message.

E. Practice. **Audio**   Listen to these examples of outgoing messages. Which are formal? Write *fml*. Which are informal? Write *infml*.

1. _____   3. _____   5. _____

2. _____   4. _____

F. (Optional) Practice.   If you have an answering machine or plan to get one, choose a style of outgoing message that is comfortable for you. Then write and record your own message.

Review: Language Functions

Answering the Phone, Asking to Take a Message, and Asking for Clarification   **Video/Audio**

Listen again to these examples of answering the phone, taking a phone message, and asking for clarification. You'll use these functions in the next section. Also, pay attention to the pronunciation of *can* and *can't*.

Put It Together

Answering the Phone, Taking a Phone Message, and Asking for Clarification   **Pair**

Work with a partner. Practice phoning each other, having short conversations, and taking messages. Alternate roles; one time Person A is the caller, and the next time Person B is the caller. Sometimes, ask to speak with your partner. Other times, ask to speak with another person who lives in your partner's home.

    To ask to speak with someone, the caller can say the following:

• Hello. May I please speak with . . . ?

• Hello. Could I speak with . . . ?

• Hi. Is . . . there? (Informal)

. : : : : Part Four Broadcast English: Gifts from the Rain Forest

Before Listening

A. Thinking Ahead. Group   You're going to listen to part of a radio program about life in the rain forest. In order to prepare for the program, discuss the answer to this question.

• What are some of the uses of rain forest plants?

Women cutting pumpkin in the South American rain forest

B. Vocabulary Preparation.   You are going to hear some new words in the radio program. First, read each sentence and guess the meaning of the underlined words. Then choose their meaning from the definitions in the box. Write the letters in the blanks.

Sentences

_____ 1. The people of the Amazon rain forest often use saplings to build their houses because they are very flexible and easy to work with.

_____ 2. Those plants are not indigenous to the area; they were brought to the region in the seventeenth century.

_____ 3. Many people worry that tourism and technology will disrupt the traditions in Mongolia and change forever the way people live.

_____ 4. They started at the coast, and it took them many days to travel to the interior of the country.

_____ 5. The radio interview of Mark Plotkin was a real revelation for me: I didn't realize that there were so many useful plants in the rain forest.

_____ 6. River blindness has always been the scourge of tropical climates, but a new drug may rid the world of that disease forever.

_____ 7. The World Health Organization is on the frontline of solving Third World health problems.

_____ 8. The people of the rain forest know how to use the plants of their ecosystem. They make medicines, food, and other useful items from the plants that live there.

_____ 9. If you were turned loose in the rain forest without any information, you probably wouldn't survive.

_____ 10. The information about the rain forest that his guide shared with him was a real eye-opener; he had never known how valuable the plants there were.

Definitions

a. (informal) surprising information

b. native

c. placed; released into

d. inland region

e. young trees

f. surprising fact

g. an interrelated system of people, plants, and animals

h. in the most advanced position; leading a battle

i. cause of great suffering

j. cause disorder in

Listening

A. Listening for the Main Idea. `Audio` This radio segment is part of a program called *Fresh Air*. In it, Marti Moss-Coane interviews enthnobotanist Mark Plotkin about his studies among tribal people in South America. It's a continuation of the radio program you heard in Chapter One. As you listen to the radio program the first time, try to answer this question:

• When Plotkin says that plants make life in the rain forest possible, what does he mean?

B. Guessing Meaning from Context. `Audio` Listen to parts of the interview and guess the meanings of the following words by paying attention to their contexts.

1. cassava = _____

2. a Maroon tribe = _____

3. malaria = _____

4. quinine = _____

C. Listening for Details. `Audio` Listen again to the interview. Listen for ways in which the people of the rain forest use the plants of their ecosystem. As you listen, list in the following chart the uses for the plant names that you hear.

Plants	Uses
palm thatch	
cassava	
forest saplings	
forest trees of the fig family	
vines	
quinine	

listening **Strategy**

Listening to an Anecdote (Audio)

An anecdote is a story or description of an incident. It often includes lots of descriptive details. It supports the main idea of what the speaker is discussing and gives the listener a clear picture of it. Paying attention to descriptive details in an anecdote helps you understand what you are listening to. Descriptive details often include adjectives that describe how people and things look and behave.

D. Listening to an Anecdote. (Audio)   Listen again to a part of the program. It includes an anecdote with lots of descriptive details. Pay attention to the descriptive language and answer these questions.

1. Why was Plotkin surprised when he met Troen?

_____

_____

2. What did Plotkin learn from Troen?

_____

_____

After Listening

A. Discussion. (Group)   Discuss the answers to these questions.

1. When Plotkin says that plants make life in the rain forest possible, what does he mean?

2. Describe the relationship of the people of the rain forest to their ecosystem. Give examples that support your explanation.

3. Describe the ecosystem that you live in and your relationship to it. How does nature play a role in your life? What plants, animals, and insects are indigenous to your community? How do you interact with them? How do you use them? How do they use you? (Note: Even if you live in a big city, think about the birds and insects that you live with.)

B. (Optional) Applying Your Knowledge.   If you have a VCR and access to a video rental store, rent *Rain Forest,* from the PBS Nature Series. It explores the fragile ecosystem of a Central American rain forest. As you watch, note why the rain forest is so important to the survival of many species.

.::::: **Part Five** Academic English: Gerald Durrell: A Modern Noah

Before Listening

A zoo in Anchorage, Alaska

The Jersey Wildlife Preservation Trust on the Island of Jersey, United Kingdom

A. Brainstorming. **Group**   Discuss what you already know about zoos with your group members by answering these questions.

1. What is the main purpose of zoos?

2. How do old-fashioned zoos compare to modern, state-of-the art zoos? Give some examples of the two types.

B. Thinking Ahead.

1. The title of the lecture is "Gerald Durrell: A Modern Noah." Who was Noah? What was he known for? What does the title suggest about Durrell?

2. Look over the main heads of the outline on pages 225–227 for the lecture. What questions do you expect (or want) the speaker to answer? Is there anything that you're curious about? Write your questions in the blanks.

_____

_____

_____

_____

3. Now look over the questions in the Comprehension Check on page 229. Are any of these similar to your own questions?

C. Guessing Meaning from Context.   In the lecture, you are going to hear some words that may be new to you. Before you listen, guess the meaning of some of the words from the lecture. The words are underlined in the sentences. Look for clues to their meaning in the words around them.

   Write your guess in the blank after each sentence. Then check your guess with your teacher or the dictionary.

1. Durrell wanted to be certain that the animals he collected would be well taken care of, so to ensure their safety, he paid his hunters more than other collectors did.

   Guess: _____

2. Jason wanted to understand the plight of the dolphin firsthand, so he spent his entire summer volunteering to work with marine biologists in Florida.

   Guess: _____

3. Many game preserves have been established as safe havens for endangered species. In them, animals are safe from hunters and poachers.

   Guess: _____

4. The board of directors' decision was <u>unanimous</u>. Everyone agreed that the zoo should be redesigned in order to provide a better environment for the animals.

Guess: _____

5. Pam spent all of her money to start a new business; the result is that she can't pay her bills and is now <u>bankrupt</u>.

Guess: _____

6. Dr. Hanson left much more than money when he died; his <u>legacy</u> includes important research that changed the way scientists do research on endangered species.

Guess: _____

Listening

A. Listening for the Main Idea. **Audio**   The lecture that you are going to hear discusses the life and achievements of Gerald Durrell. One of his accomplishments was designing a new kind of zoo in the 1950s. Listen once to the entire lecture. As you listen this time, don't take notes. Instead, follow along with the outline and keep this question in mind:

- What should the main purpose of zoos be, according to Durrell?

Note: Durrell **founded** (started) the Jersey Wildlife Preservation Trust. A "trust" in England is a non-profit organization.

Gerald Durrell

B. Guessing Meaning from Context. **Audio**   Listen to parts of the lecture again. Guess the meanings of the following words from the lecture by paying attention to their contexts.

1. perished = _____

2. humanely = _____

3. keen = _____

4. in captivity = _____

listening Strategy

Listening for Topic Signals   **Audio**

Speakers often use signals to help listeners follow and pay attention to a lecture. Listening to these signals will help you take and organize notes. One kind of signal indicates when the speaker is starting a new topic or moving on to the next subtopic of the lecture. Some of these signals include the following:

New Topic Signals

• (Now) Let's take a look at . . .

• Let's turn our attention to . . .

• This brings us to the topic of . . .

Speakers sometimes use signals to get your attention in order to make you more interested in their topic. They do this by asking a question about the topic or assuming a question on the part of the audience. (Note: They do not expect the audience to answer, especially in a formal lecture.) Here are some examples:

Attention Signals

   Why was Durrell so interested in the problem of extinction?

   You may very well wonder how Durrell funded his dream.

Speakers also use topic cues when they list items. These can be ordinal numbers or simply ordering signals.

Listing Signals

Ordinal Numbers	Ordering Signals
First,	Next,
Second,	Then,
Third,	Finally; Lastly; Last, but not least,

C. Listening for Signals. Audio

Listen again to parts of the lecture. You will hear signals like the ones in the box on page 224. As you listen to the signals, write down the signal that you hear and indicate its purpose: introduce a new topic, get attention, or list items.

1. _____

2. _____

3. _____

D. Taking Notes. Audio

This lecture is longer than the previous ones, but it is easier to understand because it deals with a person's life and accomplishments. Therefore, the outline for this lecture is less detailed than previous ones. As usual, the main topics (Roman numerals) are indicated, and there are cues for the main subtopics (capital letters). However, clues for the supporting details are missing. Listen to the entire lecture again. Take notes to complete the outline. Use the space under the capital letters to write the supporting details that *you* think are important; you will have additional chances to fill them in later.

Note: The numbered lines beneath the subtopics do not necessarily indicate the number of details that are important for you to take notes on. Use your own judgment.

Gerald Durrell: A Modern Noah

I. Introduction

    A. Durrell referred to as Noah because *of his work saving endangered species*

    _____

    B. Zoos before and after Durrell: _____

    _____

II. Durrell's Early Years

    A. Birth: _____

    B. Childhood: _____

    C. Job as zookeeper: _____

    _____

III. Zoo Professionals

    A. Other zoo professionals

        1. _____

        2. _____

        3. _____

        4. _____

B. Durrell's approach

    1. _____

    2. _____

    3. _____

    4. _____

C. Durrell's qualities

    1. _____

    2. _____

    3. _____

    4. _____

IV. Durrell's Dream

A. How he solved money problems

    1. _____

    2. _____

    3. _____

    4. _____

B. Traditional zoos

    1. _____

    2. _____

    3. _____

    4. _____

C. The problem of extinction

    1. _____

    2. _____

    3. _____

    4. _____

D. Durrell's plan (four principles)

    1. _____

    2. _____

    3. _____

    4. _____

E. The modern zoo

    1. _____

    2. _____

    3. _____

    4. _____

V. Jersey Wildlife Preservation Trust

  A. What others thought: _____

    _____

  B. What Durrell did: _____

    _____

  C. The first years: _____

    _____

  D. How he maintained the trust: _____

    _____

    1. _____

    2. _____

VI. Durrell's Legacy

  A. Died: _____

  B. His greatest legacy

    1. _____

    2. _____

E. Using Your Notes.   Answer as many of these questions as you can, either from memory or from your notes. Don't worry yet about the ones that you can't answer; you'll have another chance to listen. Work alone.

1. How did Durrell's childhood experiences include animals? _____

_____

2. Before Durrell, why did zoo animals often die a short time after capture? _____

_____

3. How did Durrell ensure that animals would be captured humanely? _____

_____

4. How did Durrell get animals used to a zoo diet? _____

_____

5. What did Durrell write about? _____

_____

6. How did Durrell deal with the problem of extinction? _____

_____

7. What were Durrell's four principles regarding zoos? _____

_____

_____

8. What were some of the problems Durrell had when he first presented his ideas for his zoo?

_____

_____

9. What problems did his zoo have in the early years? _____

_____

10. How did he solve the early problems of his zoo? _____

_____

F. Listening for Specific Information. (Audio)   Listen again to the entire lecture. This time, listen specifically for the answers to any questions that you left blank in Exercise E.

G. (Optional) Filling in the Gaps. (Audio)   Listen one last time to the entire lecture and fill in any gaps in your outline.

After Listening

A. Comprehension Check. (Pair)   Use your notes to write your answers to these questions. When you finish, compare your answers with a partner's.

1. Why is Durrell referred to as a "modern Noah"? _____

_____

2. What special qualities made Durrell good at what he did? _____

_____

3. How did Durrell earn money to start his zoo? _____

_____

4. What were zoos like before Durrell founded his own? _____

_____

5. What should the modern zoo be like, according to Durrell's vision? _____

_____

6. What is Durrell's legacy? _____

_____

B. Discussion. (Group)   Discuss the answers to these questions.

1. What should the main purpose of zoos be, according to Durrell?

2. How well do most zoos today care for animal welfare?

3. Do you enjoy going to zoos? Why or why not?

4. What are some other ways to observe animals? How do these ways compare with zoos?

Step Beyond

A. Choosing a Topic.   Choose *one* of these projects to do either by yourself or in a small group.

academic Strategy

Using a Variety of Sources and Synthesizing Information

Use a variety of sources when you prepare a presentation, even a short one. Don't rely on only one source because the information may be limited, it may have only one perspective, it may be outdated, or it may simply be wrong. Read several sources and take notes on each one. Then prepare your presentation by combining all of the information in your notes in a short summary. As you write, eliminate contradictory information or information that is not on the topic. Remember: The more you read, the better your understanding of a topic will be.

Practice.   Look at the following project assignment and the list of possible sources. Write a check (✓) next to each source that you think would be good to consult for the assignment. Then say why you think it would be a good source.

Project: Do research on the Jersey Wildlife Preservation Trust today. How is it doing? Is it prospering? Is it popular? What are the attendance figures? Is it still run according to Durrell's principles?

Possible Sources:

☐   a website on Gerald Durrell

☐   a website on the Jersey Wildlife Preservation Trust

☐   an encyclopedia entry on Gerald Durrell

☐   an encyclopedia entry on the Jersey Wildlife Preservation Trust

☐   a book about zoos written in the 1930s

☐   a book about zoos written in the 1990s

☐   a recent book about Durrell

☐   an article from a British publication about the Jersey Wildlife Preservation Trust

Project 1
Choose an endangered species—animal, plant, or insect—that interests you. Do Web or library research to find out as much as you can about the species, its habitat, reasons for its endangerment, and any attempts to save it. Present your information to the class. Bring photos of your species.

Project 2

Find out about what individuals can do to help preserve endangered species. Do research on conservation organizations, publications, ecovolunteer opportunities, and activities in which people can participate in their everyday lives. Evaluate the various opportunities and find out who is doing the best job and why. Present your findings to the class.

Project 3

Do research on the Jersey Wildlife Preservation Trust today. How is it doing? Is it prospering? Is it popular? What are the attendance figures? Is it still run according to Durrell's principles? Present your findings to the class. Bring pictures, if possible.

Project 4

Do Web or library research on the modern zoo. Find an example of a modern zoo that reflects Durrell's ideas. Alternatively, visit a nearby zoo and evaluate it according to Durrell's principles. Present your findings to the class. Bring photos, if possible.

 speaking Strategy

Eye Contact

When you give a presentation in class, make eye contact with your audience. Look at the faces of the people you are speaking to. If you are speaking to a big group, move your eyes around the room to look at everyone. Don't keep your eyes on just one member of the audience.

B. Reporting Your Information.   Organize your notes. Then give a brief report (3–5 minutes) to the class on what you have learned. Think about including pictures, charts, or any other visual material that is relevant to your topic. When you give your report, make sure you just glance at your notes; don't read them. Also, remember to make eye contact with your audience. Finally, listen carefully to your classmates' reports. Try to think of a question to ask the speaker to show that you are paying attention.

chapter Eight

Environmental Health

In this chapter, you'll read about environmental health issues. You'll also listen to information about and discuss social and environmental movements and utopias.

Part One Introduction: Healthy World, Healthy People

A. Thinking Ahead. **Pair**   Look at the photos of some environmental disasters and answer these questions.

1. What caused each of the environmental disasters in the photos?

2. How did these disasters affect the people living in or around the regions where they occurred?

3. How were these disasters **contained** (kept from spreading and cleaned up)?

4. What are these regions like today?

5. Do you know of any other environmental disasters?

Victims of the mercury poisoning disaster in Minamata, Japan

Victims of the gas disaster in Bhopal, India

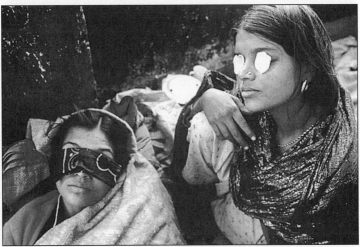

Workers measuring the level of radioactivity in Chernobyl, Russia

Houses abandoned after toxic substances percolated (passed through) to the surface in a Love Canal neighborhood in Niagara Falls, New York, USA

B. Reading.   The following article is about the challenges to human health from changes in the physical and social environment of our planet. It's by Tony McMichael, professor of epidemiology at the London School of Hygiene and Tropical Medicine.

As you read, try to answer this question:

• Can we improve environmental health? If so, how?

Healthy World, Healthy People

"The environment" is an accommodating term. Minimally, it refers to the physical and chemical conditions in the living space around us, such as the quality of local urban air, freshwater supplies, and the concentrations of chemical residues in food. A more liberal definition includes the conditions of the
5   social environment—encompassing everything from housing quality to transportation, recreational amenities, population growth, density and mobility, social networks, and political and economic equality.

From such a definition of environment flows a long list of health hazards. We are well familiar with the adverse health effects of extreme disasters such as Minamata,
10   Bhopal, Chernobyl, and Love Canal. In 1981–82, adulterated cooking oil in Spain caused about 600 deaths and serious illness in 20,000 people. Meanwhile, most environmentally induced health problems appear less obviously. They result from persistent exposure to polluted air, fecally contaminated drinking water, physical hazards, agricultural pesticides, and other toxic agents. Such exposure occurs particularly in
15   poor, powerless and under-educated Third World populations. The World Health Organization (WHO) estimates that around two-thirds of diarrheal episodes around the world—the cause of three million deaths in young children annually—arise from contaminated food or water.

These exposures are diverse, widespread, and (often) poorly documented. Their
20   health effects are often insidious. Environmental lead exposure, for example, affects young children's intelligence. Yet this public health problem—increasingly evident in traffic-congested cities in developing countries—does not figure in health and vital statistics. There are recent concerns that other widespread environmental exposures may act in non-specific fashion—for example, the compromising of the immune system
25   response that may result from our accumulating exposure to organic pesticides, or the possible effects on fertility and reproduction from the accumulation of endocrine-disrupting chemicals in the environment. Furthermore, recent research by the World Resources Institute indicates that thousands of men who were exposed to nematicide dibromochloropropane [an agricultural pesticide] in Costa Rican banana plantations

30 in the 1970s (well after it was banned in the United States) suffered from reduced fertility.

The considerable recent gains in health and longevity, first in westernized countries and subsequently in others, have resulted primarily from the reduction in early-childhood infectious disease mortality. Basic gains in food security, hygiene and water
35 sanitation, supplemented by advances in vaccination, antibiotic treatments and oral re-hydration therapy, have changed the profile of infectious disease mortality in most populations. These technical and social improvements are closely tied to the processes of urbanization, industrialization, and increasing material wealth. They, and the resultant gains in life expectancy, have therefore proceeded in parallel with increasing
40 levels of physical alteration and chemical contamination of our ambient environment.

We must now ask ourselves: For how long can we expect to maintain these parallel increasing trends in consumption, life expectancy, and environmental impact? At what stage might depletion of the world's ecological and biophysical resources strike against the health of human populations?

45 As a species, we humans are uniquely inventive, resourceful, and adaptive. The heterogeneity and flexibility of our personal behaviors, local diets, and community cultures provide a buffering against many potential adverse environmental exposures. Yet it is becoming increasingly difficult to remain optimistic about our mode of "dominant species" stewardship of this planet and our capacity to sustain healthy and happy
50 populations in the coming century.

The sheer scale of today's environmental problems will require us to take stock of our priorities and to seek socially and ecologically sustainable ways of living. Time is relatively short, the issues are complex, communities are naturally (and in some ways reassuringly) conservative, and politicians in democratic systems have limited
55 amounts of time and space. Even so, there is evidence that people instinctively understand many of these issues and, when thus confronted, will declare a primary preference for security, happiness, and health. Hence, there is an increasing public resistance to road building in Britain, to dam building in India, to logging in various Latin American countries, and to golf course construction in East Asia.

60 We must look beyond the restricted view of "environmental health" as a problem of local pollution—a problem amenable to piecemeal and technical management (but often compromised when "economic growth" is the competing value). Rather, as we acquire a more integrated view of the world's environment, its ecosystems, and their fundamental role in sustaining the health of a growing population, we must think
65 more radically about how best to manage and sustain these essential life-support systems. And at the same time, we must also maintain the immediate quality and safety of the local environment.

Source: Tony McMichael, "Healthy Word, Healthy People" from *People & the Planet* 6, no. 3, (1997). Copyright © 1997 by People & the Planet. Reprinted with the permission of the publishers.

C. Vocabulary Check.   Find words and expressions in the reading passage that mean the following:

Second paragraph:

made less pure by adding something of lower quality = _____

Third paragraph:

harmful in an unnoticeable way = _____

weakening = _____

Fourth paragraph:

giving a person fluids by mouth = _____

surrounding = _____

Sixth paragraph:

lessening the shock of something difficult = _____

care taking = _____

Seventh paragraph:

to consider carefully = _____

D. Discussion. **Group**. Discuss the answers to these questions.

1. What are some of the causes of environmentally induced health problems? What are some of the solutions?

2. Is the author of the article optimistic or pessimistic about the health of the world and its people? Find examples to support your answer.

3. Are *you* optimistic or pessimistic about the health of the world and its people? State the reasons for your answer.

E. Freewriting.   Choose *one* of these topics. Write about it for fifteen minutes. Don't worry about grammar and don't use a dictionary. Just put as many ideas as you can on paper.

• your reaction to the reading

• your predictions about the future health of the world and its people

• solutions to environmental health problems

. : ⋮ ⋮ ⋮ **Part Two** Everyday English: Environmental Health Hazards (Interview)

Before Listening

A. Predicting. [Group]
You are going to listen to Chrissy interview people on the street. She's going to ask them if they are worried about the effects of environmental hazards on their health. Make predictions about what you will hear. What kind of answers do you think that most people will give? Are most people worried about environmental health problems? If so, make predictions about what most people worry about.

B. Vocabulary Preparation: Informal Language.
The people in the interview that you'll hear use some words and expressions that are commonly found in casual conversation. First, read each sentence and guess the meaning of the underlined words. Then choose their meaning from the definitions in the box. Write the letters in the blanks.

Definitions

a. conducting or performing

b. look at; investigate

c. make an effort

d. cause a result (for) (v)

e. appearing

f. handle; cope with

g. result (n)

h. a small, raised growth (usually brown in color)

Sentences

_____ **1.** Evan, you don't have to conduct this interview—Chrissy's <u>doing</u> it.

_____ **2.** I don't know if I can help you, but I'll <u>give it a try</u>.

_____ **3.** One <u>effect</u> of getting too much sun is melanoma, or skin cancer.

_____ **4.** Environmental hazards <u>affect</u> everyone. It's impossible to avoid them.

_____ **5.** The best way to <u>deal with</u> the sun is to always cover up when you go outside.

_____ **6.** I have a strange-looking <u>mole</u> on my face, so I'm going to have the dermatologist remove it.

_____ **7.** I don't know what these strange-looking things on my skin are, so I'm going to have the doctor <u>check</u> them <u>out</u>.

_____ **8.** A lot of health issues are <u>coming up</u> that we've never seen before.

Listening

A. Listening for the Main Idea. Video/Audio   Now listen to the interview. As you listen, try to answer this question:

• Do most people worry about environmental health hazards?

When you finish listening, circle your answer: *Yes* or *No*

B. Listening for Details. Video/Audio   Listen to the interview again. Fill in the chart for each speaker. Is the speaker worried about environmental health hazards? Circle *yes* or *no.*

Then listen again for the answer to this question: If the speaker is worried, what is he or she worried about?

Speaker	Worried?		What Is He or She Worried about?
1	(Yes)	No	quality of air and food
2	Yes	No	
3	Yes	No	
4	Yes	No	
5	Yes	No	
6	Yes	No	
7	Yes	No	

listening Strategy

Listening for Emotions Audio

You can often hear emotion in a speaker's voice. Emotion is expressed in a person's voice by tone (warm, cold), pitch (high, low), and rate of speech (fast, slow). You can get further information about a person's emotions by watching his or her facial expressions (laughing, smiling, frowning) and body movements (hand and arm gestures). All these indicators convey meanings such as excitement, nervousness, or fear. The absence of these indicators can mean that the person wants to sound unemotional, or neutral.

C. Listening for Emotions. Video/Audio   Listen to (and watch, if possible) the interviews again. Try to determine each speaker's emotional state by using cues such as tone, pitch, rate, laughter, facial expressions, and body movements to determine his or her emotions. Circle the emotion that you hear for each speaker, or add your own if none in the list matches.

Speaker	Emotions					(Other)
1	neutral	calm	nervous	concerned	scared	_____
2	neutral	calm	nervous	concerned	scared	_____
3	neutral	calm	nervous	concerned	scared	_____
4	neutral	calm	nervous	concerned	scared	_____
5	neutral	calm	nervous	concerned	scared	_____
6	neutral	calm	nervous	concerned	scared	_____
7	neutral	calm	nervous	concerned	scared	_____

After Listening

A. Taking a Survey. **Class**   Move around the classroom and interview other students. (In addition, for homework your teacher might have you interview other people in your school or neighborhood.) Ask people these questions.

• Are you worried about the effects of environmental hazards on your health? If so, what are you concerned about?

Take notes on your survey using a chart like the one on this page.

Survey: Environmental Hazards
Total number of people you asked: _____
Total number of people who said that they are worried: _____
Examples of concerns:

B. Discussing Survey Results. **Pair**   Discuss the results of your survey with a partner. Did any of the concerns surprise you?

. : : : : : **Part Three** The Mechanics of Listening
and Speaking

Language Functions

Expressing Concern `Audio`

There are several ways to express concern or worry. Here are some examples:

- <u>I'm concerned about</u> overpopulation.
- <u>I'm worried about</u> overpopulation.
- <u>I worry about</u> overpopulation.
- <u>My main concern is that</u> there are too many people in the world.
- <u>I'm afraid that</u> because of overpopulation, we'll run out of resources.

Your tone can remain neutral when you make statements of concern; in fact, in an academic setting, it's often a good idea not to sound emotional in discussions.

Intensifying Concern `Audio`

You can add the adverbs *rather, quite, very, really,** or *extremely* to statements with *be* + adjective (*concerned, worried*) to intensify your concern:

I'm <u>rather</u> concerned about overpopulation.   **Weaker**

I'm <u>quite</u> concerned about overpopulation.

I'm <u>very</u> concerned about overpopulation.

I'm <u>really</u> concerned about overpopulation.

I'm <u>extremely</u> worried about overpopulation.   **Stronger**

Your tone is still neutral, but the intensifier indicates the seriousness of the situation.

*Really is used mainly in informal situations.

A. Practice. **Audio**   Listen for intensity in these statements of concern. If you hear a statement that doesn't sound intense, circle *not intense*. If you hear a statement that sounds intense, circle *intense*.

1.	Not intense	Intense	**5.**	Not intense	Intense
2.	Not intense	Intense	**6.**	Not intense	Intense
3.	Not intense	Intense	**7.**	Not intense	Intense
4.	Not intense	Intense	**8.**	Not intense	Intense

Stress

Intensifying with Stress **Audio**

You can also intensify a concern with stress. To do this, you stress the intensifying adverb (*very, quite, extremely, really*). When you intensify with stress, you reveal emotion. This is appropriate in many situations, such as in personal discussions and when you want to motivate your listeners to act. Here are some examples:

I'm *very* concerned about bad drinking water.

I'm *extremely* worried about my grades.

B. Practice. **Audio**   Listen to the following statements of concern. Listen for their emotional intensity. If you hear a neutral statement, circle *neutral*. If you hear an emotional statement with a stressed adverb, circle *emotional*.

1.	Neutral	Emotional	**5.**	Neutral	Emotional
2.	Neutral	Emotional	**6.**	Neutral	Emotional
3.	Neutral	Emotional	**7.**	Neutral	Emotional
4.	Neutral	Emotional	**8.**	Neutral	Emotional

C. Practice. **Pair**   Work with a partner. Express concern about the following issues. If you feel intense concern about an issue, use an adverb and/or stress to intensify it. If you *aren't* concerned, make a negative statement. (Example: <u>I'm not concerned/I'm not very concerned about</u> grades.) Ask for and give a reason for each concern.

Issues

1. the environment

2. having a career and a family

3. getting sick

4. grades

5. making enough money

6. AIDS

7. overpopulation

8. getting old

9. finding love

10. your concerns: _____

_____

_____

Pronunciation

/ɛ/, /æ/, and /ə/   **Audio**

It's important to pronounce the sounds /ɛ/, /æ/, and /ə/ carefully. People may not understand you if you don't pronounce words with these sounds correctly.
Here are some examples:

/ɛ/	/æ/	/ə/
The tr<u>e</u>k is long.	The tr<u>a</u>ck is long.	The tr<u>u</u>ck is long.

Here are more examples:

/ɛ/	/æ/	/ə/
b<u>e</u>t	b<u>a</u>t	b<u>u</u>t
b<u>e</u>d	b<u>a</u>d	b<u>u</u>d
s<u>e</u>nd	s<u>a</u>nd	s<u>u</u>nned
l<u>e</u>g	l<u>a</u>g	l<u>u</u>g
fl<u>e</u>sh	fl<u>a</u>sh	fl<u>u</u>sh
d<u>ea</u>d	d<u>a</u>d	d<u>u</u>d
t<u>e</u>n	t<u>a</u>n	t<u>o</u>n

Notice the two ways of spelling the /ɛ/ sound and the /ə/ sound.

D. Practice. (Audio) Listen to the following words. Circle the word that you hear.

1. send   sand   sunned   7. hem   ham   hum

2. leg   lag   lug   8. pen   pan   pun

3. trek   track   truck   9. kept   capped   cupped

4. flesh   flash   flush   10. mess   mass   muss

5. dead   dad   dud   11. beg   bag   bug

6. mesh   mash   mush   12. better   batter   butter

E. Practice. (Audio) Check (✓) the statement that you hear.

1. _____ a. That's a funny pen.   4. _____ a. It's just a short trek.

   _____ b. That's a funny pan.   _____ b. It's just a short track.

   _____ c. That's a funny pun.   _____ c. It's just a short truck.

2. _____ a. Is that better?   5. _____ a. I kept it.

   _____ b. Is that batter?   _____ b. I capped it.

   _____ c. Is that butter?   _____ c. I cupped it.

3. _____ a. Do you have a ten?

   _____ b. Do you have a tan?

   _____ c. Do you have a ton?

F. Practice. (Pair) Say one of the statements from Exercise E. (Don't say them in order.) Your partner will write *a*, *b*, or *c*. Check to see if the statement matches the one you said. If your partner didn't write the correct letter, try again. Then exchange roles.

G. Practice. **Class**   Now use words with the sounds /ɛ/, /æ/, and /ə / in conversations. Ask questions to fill in the chart on this page or use the Word List below it to make up your own. Which student collects the most names?

Find someone who . . .	Names
likes to get a t<u>a</u>n	
has ever been on a tr<u>e</u>k in the mountains	
knows a good p<u>u</u>n	
has a favorite p<u>e</u>n	
knows how to s<u>a</u>nd wood	
collected b<u>u</u>gs as a child	
likes m<u>a</u>shed potatoes	
has driven a tr<u>u</u>ck	
your question:	

Word List					
send	sand	sunned	leg	lag	lug
trek	track	truck	flesh	flash	flush
dead	dad	dud	mesh	mash	mush
hem	ham	hum	pen	pan	pun
kept	capped	cupped	mess	mass	muss
beg	bag	bug	better	batter	butter

Review: Language Functions

Expressing Concern (Video/Audio)

Listen again to these examples of expressing concern. As you listen, pay attention to intensity. Also, listen for words with the /ɛ/, /æ/, and /ə/ sounds. You'll use these functions in the next section.

Put It Together

A. Talking about Concerns. (Pair)   Find a partner. Ask your partner about his or her most important concerns in life. As you answer, use the expressions for expressing concern, intensifiers, and stress, if appropriate. Give reasons if your partner asks for them. As you speak, try to pronounce the /ɛ/, /æ/, and /ə/ sounds correctly.

When you are finished, find another partner. Talk to as many classmates as you can. Discuss the following. Are you worried about

School/Career

• Getting good grades?

• Getting a good job when you finish your education?

• Making enough money?

Friends and Love

- Making friends?

- Finding the love of your life?

Family

- Having children and raising a family?

- Being able to have a family and a successful career?

Health

- Your health?

- The health of parents or other family members?

The World/The Environment

- Conflict between national or ethnic groups?

- The environment and the future of the planet?

B. Discussion. **Group**   In groups, **rank** (put in order) the top three concerns of your class members. Discuss these concerns and ways to deal with them.

. . : : ! ! **Part Four** Broadcast English: A Utopian Community

Before Listening

A. Thinking Ahead. **Group**   You're going to listen to part of a radio program about a model community in Colombia called Gaviotas. In order to prepare for the program, discuss the answers to these questions.

- What is your idea of a **utopia** (an ideal place, especially one with ideal social conditions)?

- Describe some utopias, real or in literature, that you have read or heard about.

B. Vocabulary Preparation.   In the radio program, you are going to hear some words that may be new to you. First, read each sentence and guess the meaning of the underlined words. Then choose their meaning from the definitions in the box. Write the letters in the blanks.

Sentences

_____ **1.** They were true <u>visionaries</u>: They had an idea for a perfect community—one that had never before existed—and they were able to realize it with the help of some friends.

_____ **2.** The area was not fit for human <u>habitation</u> because the water and land were polluted, so the pioneers had to move on to a new place.

_____ **3.** There's nothing in that part of the country—no trees, plants, or water—just <u>desolate</u> plains.

_____ **4.** The small boy took some broad leaves and showed us how to <u>fashion</u> hats from them.

_____ **5.** We traveled thirty miles in a deeply <u>rutted</u> road. The road was so bumpy that we ruined the tires.

_____ **6.** His dream was to retire, go back to his homeland in Colombia, and buy a big <u>hacienda</u>.

_____ **7.** Jason made a paper airplane, but because it wasn't <u>aerodynamic</u>, it wouldn't fly.

_____ **8.** This device allows you to <u>tap</u> drinking water from a barrel.

_____ **9.** <u>Protocol</u> does not allow him to shake the emperor's hand; he must bow instead.

_____ **10.** They didn't follow the rules in this community, so they were <u>ostracized</u>. They finally left because no one would speak to them.

> **Definitions**
>
> *a.* with deep, narrow tracks
>
> *b.* deserted
>
> *c.* living in a certain place
>
> *d.* remove (a liquid)
>
> *e.* a system of fixed rules for behavior
>
> *f.* people who have ideal goals for the future but do not necessarily have the means to realize them
>
> *g.* make
>
> *h.* designed for movement through the air
>
> *i.* socially excluded
>
> *j.* Spanish word for "ranch"

Listening

Colombia

Gaviotas

A. Listening for the Main Idea. (Audio)   This radio segment is part of a National Public Radio series on "Searching for Solutions." In it, Alan Weisman reports on Gaviotas, a model community in eastern Colombia. The community is a social and environmental utopia. As you listen to the radio program the first time, try to answer this question:

• In what ways is Gaviotas a utopia, or model community?

 *listening* Strategy

Recognizing Figurative Language (Audio)

Many words can be used two ways: *literally* and *figuratively*. A literal meaning is the most common and usually the first one listed in the dictionary. A figurative meaning is different from the usual meaning; it often makes a word picture or a comparison. If you know the literal meaning of a word, it helps you guess its meaning when it's used figuratively. Here is an example for the word *fresh*:

• Let's get some <u>fresh</u> fruit at the market. (Here, *fresh* is used literally; it means "food or produce that's in good condition or newly caught, picked, or prepared.")

• His ideas are <u>fresh</u> and surprising. (*Fresh* is used figuratively here; it means "new or different.")

B. Recognizing Figurative Uses of Words. (Audio)   Listen to parts of the program and guess the figurative meanings of the following words. Use your knowledge of their literal meanings (given in the following list) and their contexts to guess. Write your guesses in the blanks.

Literal Meanings

bright = full of light; shining

oasis = a place with trees and water in the desert

flourish = to grow healthily, especially a plant

stale = no longer fresh; not good to eat or smell

1. bright = _____

2. oasis = _____

3. flourishing = _____

4. stale = _____

C. Listening for Details. (Audio) Listen again to part of the program. Listen for the answers to these questions about the innovative technology at Gaviotas. Write the answers in the blanks.

1. What is special or unusual about the solar panels at Gaviotas?

_____

_____

2. What use does the stationary bicycle have?

_____

_____

3. What's special or different about the double-action pump?

_____

_____

_____

_____

4. What are the children on the seesaw actually doing?

_____

_____

_____

_____

Children at the Gaviotas Daycare Center

D. Listening for Implicit Reasons. (Audio)   As you saw in Chapter Two, speakers don't always state a reason clearly with a word such as *because*. Instead, they simply imply a reason in the context. Listen to excerpts from the radio program. Listen for the implied reasons for the following:

1. Why did the founders of Gaviotas choose the "hardest place" to establish their community?

_____

_____

2. Why are there no "crimes of passion" or adultery in Gaviotas?

_____

_____

After Listening

speaking Strategy

Taking Turns

When you speak in a group, it's important to take turns. If you like to talk, make sure that you give the quieter group members a chance to speak. You can help them by asking them for their opinions. If you don't like to talk, force yourself to make at least one comment. If you are shy, sometimes it helps to write down your ideas first and then say them.

A. Discussion. (Group)   Discuss the answers to these questions.

1. In what ways is Gaviotas a utopia, or model community?

2. What does Paolo Lugari mean when he says: "All our development models have been created in countries with four seasons, with totally different conditions from tropical countries. When we import solutions from northern countries, not only don't we solve our problems, but we import theirs"?

3. Why do Gaviotans have a hard time marketing their inventions?

4. Why is there no crime in Gaviotas?

5. Does Gaviotas sound like paradise to you? Would you like to live there? Why or why not?

B. (Optional) Applying Your Knowledge.   Look for examples of people creating or using environmentally appropriate technology or products in your community. Look for the following:

- Are solar panels common?

- Do you see windmills anywhere?

- Is there a recycling program?

- Do you see many electric cars?

- Are there shops that specialize in environmentally safe products such as un-dyed clothing and nontoxic cleansers?

- What other signs do you see in your community of people trying to live in harmony with nature?

Find out about the advantages and disadvantages of these technologies and products. If possible, ask people if they are satisfied with these technologies and products, and if not, why not? Report your findings to the class and discuss the issues that prevent people from living a more ecologically sound lifestyle.

. : : : : : **Part Five** Academic English:
                       The Green Movement

Before Listening

A. Brainstorming. Group   In this chapter, you are going to listen to a discussion section instead of a lecture. Teaching assistants (T. A.s) conduct discussion sections so students can talk about a professor's lecture and the accompanying reading material. T. A.s also give assignments and quizzes and generally help students understand difficult material.

The lecture that this group will be discussing is on the Green Movement. Before you listen, discuss what you already know about the Green Movement (also known as Greens, or the Green Party in some countries). Answer these questions.

- What does the Green Movement believe in?

- What countries have strong Green parties?

B. Thinking Ahead. The outline on pages 258–259 reflects the lecture that the students in the discussion section heard. Many students didn't take complete notes, or didn't understand the lecture completely. Looking at the incomplete outline, what questions do you expect the students to have? Write their questions in the blanks.

_____

_____

_____

_____

_____

C. Guessing Meaning from Context.   Guess the meaning of some of the words from the discussion. The words are underlined in the sentences. Look for clues to their meaning in the words around them.

Write your guess in the blank after each sentence. Compare your answers with a partner's. Then check your guess with your teacher or the dictionary.

1. Today I'm going over the material you read in Chapter Ten. I'll begin by explaining the chart on page 125.

   Guess: _____

2. Instead of just analyzing one department in the organization, let's take a holistic view; that way we can see how each department interacts with the organization as a whole.

   Guess: _____

3. Instead of telling you the whole story, I'll just give it to you <u>in a nutshell</u>: I had a problem with my car and that's why I'm late.

   Guess: _____

4. I don't know where that strange custom came from; it must <u>be rooted in</u> some ancient ritual that no one remembers anymore.

   Guess: _____

5. He has some <u>wacky</u> idea about going to live on some commune in Colombia, but I think he's crazy!

   Guess: _____

6. That school is a good place for kids who are <u>misfits</u>, you know, the ones who just don't fit in anywhere.

   Guess: _____

Listening

A. Listening for the Main Idea. **Audio**   Listen once to the discussion. (You'll listen again later.) As you listen this time, don't take notes. Instead, follow along with the outline and try to answer this question:

- What is the philosophy of the Green Movement?

listening Strategy

Listening to Accented English **Audio**

Many T. A.s in the United States and Canada are nonnative speakers. Sometimes you may not understand them because, like many people—including native speakers—you have gotten used to hearing standard English accents. When you can't understand a word or expression that you hear in a different accent, follow these steps:

1. First, decide if it's necessary for the overall meaning of what you are listening to. If it isn't, forget about it. If it is, go to Number 2.

2. Supply the missing word, expression, or idea with the most logical possibility, based on the context.

   Here is an example:

   If someone says,

   > "The considerable recent gains in health and *longevity,* first in westernized countries and subsequently in others, have resulted primarily from the *reduction* in early-childhood [unintelligible expression]."

   you can guess that the missing part has something to do with death or disease, because that's the obvious reason that people would be living longer. (The hints are *longevity* and *reduction.*)

3. If you don't understand the overall meaning, and can't guess the missing word or expression, ask the person to repeat what he or she just said.

B. Taking Notes. **Audio**   Listen to the discussion again. As you have seen, the outline is **skeletal** (missing a lot of details). Listen carefully to the T. A. and to the students' questions. Notice that the T. A. is a nonnative speaker. Use the strategy on pages 257–258 to guess words and expressions that you don't understand. Take notes to complete the outline.

The Green Movement

I. Ecotopia: Origins of the Concept

   A. Utopia _____

       _____

   B. Ecology _____

       _____

   C. Ecotopia _____

       _____

II. The Green Movement

   A. Philosophy _____

       _____

   B. Ten key values of the U.S. Green Movement

      1. _____

      2. _____

3. _____

4. _____

5. _____

6. _____

7. _____

8. _____

9. _____

10. _____

III. Conclusion _____

_____

_____

_____

C. Important Details.

Before doing the next listening exercise, fill in as many of these blanks as you can, either from memory or from your notes. Don't worry yet about the ones you can't answer; you'll have another chance to listen.

• What do these "key values" of the U.S. Green Movement mean?

1. ecological wisdom = _____

2. grassroots democracy = _____

3. personal and social responsibility = _____

4. nonviolence = _____

5. decentralization = _____

6. community-based economics = _____

7. feminism = _____

8. respect for diversity = _____

9. global responsibility = _____

10. future focus/sustainability = _____

D. Listening Again for Important Details. (Audio)   Go back to the beginning of Exercise C. Listen again to the part of the discussion that explains the ten values. Either check your answers or fill in missing answers.

academic Strategy

Memorizing (Audio)

In academic settings, you often have to memorize lists of concepts or definitions. Everyone has his or her favorite memory tricks, such as associating a word with something it reminds you of.

A good way to memorize a group of concepts or words and their definitions is to make flashcards using index cards. Write the word or concept on one side of the card and the definition on the back. Show yourself the word, define it, then flip it over to see if you're right. Mix the cards up every time you study.

Practice.   Use index cards to study the ten key values, the vocabulary from this chapter, or anything else you want to remember. Try to memorize the material. Use your favorite memory tricks. Get a partner, and then test each other. Then discuss the memory tricks you used.

Note: Memory tricks tend to be personal; other people's may only work for them.

E. (Optional) Filling in the Gaps. (Audio)   Listen one last time to the entire discussion and fill in any gaps in your outline.

After Listening

A. Comprehension Check. (Pair)   Use your notes to write your answers to these questions. When you finish, compare your answers with a partner's.

1. What's an ecotopia?

_____

_____

2. What is the book *Ecotopia* about?

_____

_____

3. What's the relationship between the book *Ecotopia* and the Green Movement, according to the lecture discussion?

    _____

    _____

4. State the basic philosophy of the Green Movement in your own words.

    _____

    _____

5. When did the Green Movement begin in the United States?

    _____

    _____

B. Discussion. Group Discuss the answers to these questions.

1. What do the Greens mean when they say that "environmental and social problems are all connected" and that "they must be solved in a holistic fashion"?

2. Are Greens realistic? Are they having any effect on the world?

Step Beyond

A. Choosing a Topic. Choose *one* of these projects to do either by yourself or in a small group.

Project 1

Do Web or library research to find recent news articles on the Green Movement and learn about some of its recent activities. Alternately, find out more about the history of the Green Movement. Who started it? Where did it start? Who or what influenced the formation of the movement? How strong is it in your country? In other countries?

Project 2

Do Web or library research to find recent news articles about Gaviotas today. How is the community doing now? Have there been any changes since the 1994 radio program that you listened to? If so, what are they? What does the future hold for this community?

Project 3

Do research on other utopias (or model communities) in history, such as Agapemone, founded in England in 1849 or New Harmony, established in Kansas (United States) in 1825 or Oneida Community in New York State. Compare one of these to Gaviotas.

Project 4

Do research on a mythical utopia such as Camelot or Atlantis or on a literary utopia such as those in *The Lost Horizon* by James Hilton or *Erewhon* by Samuel Butler. Compare one of these to Gaviotas.

B. Reporting Your Information.   Organize your notes. Then give a brief report (3–5 minutes) to the class on what you have learned. Think about including pictures, charts, or any other visual material that is relevant to your topic. When you give your report, make sure you just glance at your notes— don't read them. Remember to make eye contact with your audience. Also, listen carefully to your classmates' reports. Try to think of a question to ask the speaker to show that you are paying attention.

Instructions for Information Gaps

These pages contain the information for Student B in the info gap activities.

Chapter Two, Part Two, After Listening

Exercise C, Page 42

Student B   **Primate Family Tree**

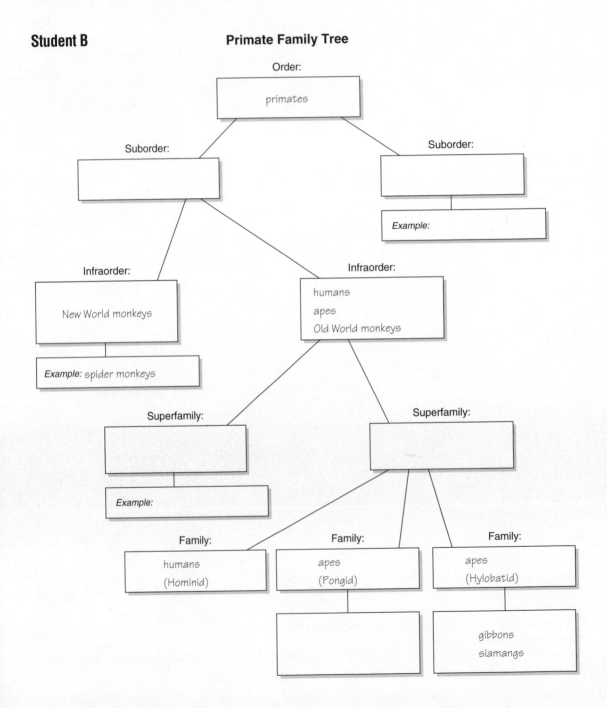

Chapter Seven, Part Two, After Listening   Exercise A, Pages 209 and 210

Student B

Endangered Species: Where in the World?

Endangered Species	Habitat	Reasons for Endangerment
Giant panda	China	
Cheetah	A small portion in the Middle East (mostly Iran) and parts of East and South Africa	
	Hawaiian Islands	• Cattle grazing • Urban development
		• Loss of habitat due to development
Blue karner butterfly	North America: Wisconsin, Indiana, Michigan, Minnesota, New Hampshire, New York, and Illinois	
	Russia, China, South Korea, and Japan	• Loss of habitat • Drainage of wetlands • Human interference
European tree frog		• Disappearance of wetlands
Short horned lizard	North America: Southern Canada to Mexico and from eastern Kansas to western Oregon and Washington	
	Coastal waters of Florida and Georgia	• Collisions with boats causing injury or death • Entanglement in fishing lines or other litter • Pollution of food source (grasses)
Fin whale	All oceans of the world	

Source: Table: "Endangered Species: Where in the World?" adapted from a website produced by the IWC Volunteer Webweaver Team. Available from http://iwc.org/volunteers/archives/May98/; INTERNET. Copyright © 1998 by the International Wildlife Coalition. Reprinted with permission.

appendix
Common Irregular Verbs

be am-is-are, was-were, been
beat, beat, beaten
become, became, become
begin, began, begun
bend, bent, bent
bet, bet, bet
bleed, bled, bled
blow, blew, blown
break, broke, broken
bring, brought, brought
build, built, built
burst, burst, burst
buy, bought, bought
catch, caught, caught
choose, chose, chosen
come, came, come
cost, cost, cost
creep, crept, crept
cut, cut, cut
dig, dug, dug
dive, dove *or* dived, dived
do, did, done
draw, drew, drawn
drink, drank, drunk
drive, drove, driven
eat, ate, eaten
fall, fell, fallen
feed, fed, fed
feel, felt, felt
fight, fought, fought
find, found, found
fit, fit, fit
flee, fled, fled
fly, flew, flown
forget, forgot, forgotten

freeze, froze, frozen
get, got, got *or* gotten
give, gave, given
go, went, gone
grind, ground, ground
grow, grew, grown
hang, hung, hung
have, had, had
hear, heard, heard
hide, hid, hidden
hit, hit, hit
hold, held, held
hurt, hurt, hurt
keep, kept, kept
know, knew, known
lay, laid, laid
lead, led, led
leave, left, left
lend, lent, lent
let, let, let
lie, lay, lain
lose, lost, lost
make, made, made
mean, meant, meant
meet, met, met
pay, paid, paid
put, put, put
read, read, read
ride, rode, ridden
ring, rang, rung
rise, rose, risen
run, ran, run
say, said, said
see, saw, seen
sell, sold, sold
send, sent, sent

set, set, set
sew, sewed, sewn
shake, shook, shaken
shine, shone, shone
shoot, shot, shot
show, showed, shown
shrink, shrank, shrunk
shut, shut, shut
sing, sang, sung
sink, sank, sunk
sit, sat, sat
sleep, slept, slept
speak, spoke, spoken
spend, spent, spent
split, split, split
spread, spread, spread
stand, stood, stood
steal, stole, stolen
stick, stuck, stuck
strike, struck, struck
swear, swore, sworn
sweep, swept, swept
swim, swam, swum
take, took, taken
teach, taught, taught
tear, tore, torn
tell, told, told
think, thought, thought
throw, threw, thrown
understand, understood, understood
wake, woke *or* waked, waked
wear, wore, worn
win, won, won
wind, wound, wound
write, wrote, written

credits

Unit Openers ©PhotoDisc, Inc.

Photo Credits

Chapter 1. Opener: ©CORBIS/Charles & Josette Lenars; p. 4 (top): ©James Blair/NGS Image Collection; p. 4 (bottom): ©Breck P. Kent/Animals Animals; p. 5: ©James Blair/NGS Image Collection; p. 8, 14: ©The McGraw-Hill Companies, Inc.; p. 17 (top left): ©Superstock; p. 17 (bottom left): ©Victor Englebert/Photo Researchers; p. 17 (right): ©Dr. Mark J. Plotkin; p. 25: ©CORBIS/Christel Gerstenberg; p. 26: ©V. Sadchikov/TASS/Sovfoto/Eastfoto

Chapter 2. Opener: ©Superstock; p. 34: ©Twentieth Century Fox/The Kobal Collection; p. 35: ©Susan Kuklin/Photo Researchers; p. 36 (top): ©Ron Cohn/The Gorilla Foundation; p. 36 (bottom): ©PhotoDisc; p. 37: ©John Warden/Superstock; p. 39: ©The McGraw-Hill Companies, Inc.; p. 42 (left): ©PhotoDisc; p. 42 (right): ©John Warden/Superstock; p. 43 (top—both): ©PhotoDisc; p. 43 (bottom left): ©Renee Lynn/Photo Researchers; p. 43 (bottom right): ©PhotoDisc; p. 49: ©The McGraw-Hill Companies, Inc.; p. 53: ©CORBIS/Karl Ammann

Chapter 3. Opener: ©Michael Mortimer Robinson/Superstock; p. 74: ©The McGraw-Hill Companies, Inc.; p. 76: Salvador Dali. *Daddy Longlegs of the Evening—Hope!* 1940. ©1999 Artists Rights Society (ARS), New York/Private Collection/Superstock; p. 86: ©The McGraw-Hill Companies, Inc.; p. 88: ©Angela Rowlings/AP/Wide World Photos; p. 100: ©Dennis Yankus/Superstock; p. 101: Edvard Munch. *Self-Portrait in Weimar.* ©1999 The Munch Museum, Oslo, Norway/The Munch-Ellingsen Group/Artists Rights Society (ARS), New York/Superstock

Chapter 4. Opener: ©Culver Pictures/Superstock; p. 111 (top): ©The Kobal Collection; p. 111 (bottom): ©United Artist/The Kobal Collection; p. 112, 119: ©The McGraw-Hill Companies, Inc.

Chapter 5. Opener: ©PhotoDisc; p. 136: Courtesy Grameen Bank, photo courtesy of Microcredit Summit Secretariat, Washington, D.C.; p. 137 (top): Courtesy Association d'Appui aux Conducteurs de Chariots du Zaire, photo courtesy of Microcredit Summit Secretariat, Washington, D.C.; p. 137 (bottom): Courtesy ADEMI, photo courtesy of Microcredit Summit Secretariat,

Washington, D.C.; p. 139, 148: ©The McGraw-Hill Companies, Inc.; p. 149 (left): ©PhotoDisc; p. 149 (right): ©CORBIS/Albrecht G. Schaefer; p. 153: ©CORBIS/Julia Waterlow/Eye Ubiquitous; p. 156: ©CORBIS/Bettmann; p. 154: ©AP/Wide World Photos

Chapter 6. Opener, p. 164 (top): ©Reuters/Claro Cortes/Archive Photos; p. 164 (bottom left): ©CORBIS/Dave G. Houser; p. 164 (bottom right): ©Andy Hernandez/Liaison Agency; p. 165: ©1999 Star Tribune/Minneapolis-St. Paul; p. 169, 175: ©The McGraw-Hill Companies, Inc.; p. 177 (left): ©John Spaull/Panos Pictures; p. 177 (right): ©C. Patricia Lanza; p. 179: ©CORBIS/Ed Eckstein; p. 188: ©Reuters/Claro Cortes/Archive Photos

Chapter 7. Opener; Alan D. Carey/Photo Researchers; p. 200 (beetle): ©CORBIS/Susan Middleton & David Liitschwager; p. 200 (crane): ©Tom McHugh/Photo Researchers; p. 200 (bobcat): ©PhotoDisc; p. 201 (urchin): ©PhotoDisc; p. 201 (crocodile): ©Mark Moulton/Photo Researchers; p. 201 (killfish): ©Steinhart Aquarium/Tom McHugh/Photo Researchers; p. 201 (loris): ©PhotoDisc; p. 201 (macaw): ©Luiz C. Marigo/Peter Arnold; p. 201 (elephant): ©PhotoDisc; p. 202, 203: ©PhotoDisc; p. 206, 2316: ©The McGraw-Hill Companies, Inc.; p. 217: ©Sean Sprague/Stock Boston; p. 221 (top): ©CORBIS/Douglas Peebles; p. 221 (bottom): ©Durrell Wildlife Conservation Trust, Photo by Phillip Coffey; p. 223: ©Durrell Wildlife Conservation Trust, Photo by Peter Trenchard

Chapter 8. Opener: ©Jeremy Horner/Panos Pictures; p. 234 (top): ©CORBIS/Michael S. Yamashita; p. 234 (bottom): ©Pablo Bartholomew/Liaison Agency; p. 235 (top): ©Gamma Moscou/Liaison Agency; p. 235 (bottom): ©Galen Rowell/CORBIS; p. 240, 248: ©The McGraw-Hill Companies, Inc.; p. 251, 252: ©Antonin Kratochvil; p. 255: ©Douglas Burrows/Liaison Agency

Radio Credits

Chapter 1 and Chapter 7. Excerpt from interview with ethnobotanist Mark Plotkin, author of *Tales of a Shaman's Apprentice* on "Fresh Air" (Marti Moss-Coane, interviewer), September 21, 1993, WHYY, Philadelphia. Copyright ©1993 by WHYY, Inc. and Fresh Air. Used with permission.